# Virtue's End

*Classici della filosofia contemporanea*

Regione Siciliana
Assessorato ai Beni Culturali ed Ambientali ed alla Pubblica Istruzione

## Other Titles of Interest from St. Augustine's Press and Dumb Ox Books

# Virtue's End

## God in the Moral Philosophy of Aristotle and Aquinas

Edited by
Fulvio Di Blasi, Joshua P. Hochschild, and Jeffrey Langan

ST. AUGUSTINE'S PRESS
South Bend, Indiana
2008

In association with

Thomas International

Manufactured in the United States of America.

1  2  3  4  5  6    14  13  12  11  10  09  08

**Library of Congress Cataloging in Publication Data**
Virtue's end : God in the moral philosophy of Aristotle and Aquinas /
edited by Fulvio Di Blasi, Joshua P. Hochschild, and Jeffrey Langan.
p.  cm.
Includes bibliographical references.
ISBN-13: 978-1-58731-901-3 (paperbound: alk. paper)
ISBN-10: 1-58731-901-2 (paperbound: alk. paper)
1. Aristotle. 2. Aristotle. Nicomachean ethics. 3. Thomas, Aquinas, Saint,
1225?–1274 – Ethics. 4. God.  I. Di Blasi, Fulvio.
II. Hochschild, Joshua P., 1972–  III. Langan, Jeffrey, 1970–
B491.G63V57 2007
170.9 – dc22        2007030830

∞ The paper used in this publication meets the minimum requirements of the American National Standard for Information Sciences – Permanence of Paper for Printed Materials, ANSI Z39.48–1984.

ST. AUGUSTINE'S PRESS
www.staugustine.net

# TABLE OF CONTENTS

# PREFACE

The first and fundamental moral guidelines are self-evidently true. If "good" means the desirable, it is immediately obvious that good should be done and evil avoided. The good thus recognized is not the end of this activity or that; it is the fulfilment or perfection of the agent as such not yet discriminated into its constituents. The pursuit of the objects of instinctive desires – food and drink, venereal pleasure – will be human to the degree that such pursuits are brought under the pursuit of our overall fulfillment. Even the pursuit of knowledge must be subservient to that overall good. Thus, it is not a matter of orchestrating particular or "basic" goods, brokering their claims lest one be pursued at the expense of the others. Rather, particular goods are regulated by our overall good which turns out to be a common good in several senses. It is common to, comprehensive of, all the basic goods, and it is a good we share with others since we are by nature familial and political animals.

Forgive this cryptic recall of the basic assumptions of natural law. These assumptions seem to call into question the assumptions of this collection of essays. How so?

If theism is essential to morality, knowledge of God must be present from the very beginning.

But that there is a God is not *per se notum*, as are the most common principles of natural law.

Thus God cannot be invoked at the outset.

This would suggest that knowledge of God and his role in our moral lives comes later and that in turn suggests that the moral life gets under way without reference to the existence of God.

Well, as we say in the trade, *distinguo*.

The theory or account of natural law is not identical with what it is a theory or account of. If I should say that natural law consists of the first self-evident principles of practical reasoning or, alternatively, that natural law is the peculiarly human participation in divine law, I am, in both cases, offering an account. But one can know the precepts of natural law without being able to understand either one of those accounts. They come later. They presuppose what they are about.

Accordingly, to say that natural law implies theism could mean that an adequate account of natural law is going to have to take into account God's role in the world and in our lives.

Or it could be taken to mean that any recognition of moral precepts is a recognition of God.

Here again, *distinguo*.

When Thomas Aquinas is considering the claim of some that God's existence is self-evident to us, he allows that in some sense God is known right off. This can be seen, he suggests, in the desire for happiness, which is the rock bottom assumption of natural law. If happiness is our total good and God is total goodness then in pursuing happiness we are in some sense pursuing God. But you can only pursue something if you know it. So in some sense we must know God from the outset. And so we do. We know God in knowing that we want to be happy, that is, implicitly.

Now, it could be said that the most common precepts of natural law are also known implicitly just as the first principles of reasoning as such are known implicitly. The principle of contradiction is grasped in judgments of a very concrete sort. The sun is shining or it is not. It is because this is true thanks to something not confined to the sun that, in making the judgment, we are not simply uttering a particular truth, a regional truth, so to say. So too, if being is the first thing grasped by the human mind, it does not seem to be the first noun uttered. Being is first grasped in very concrete instances and what will become specific or even proper names have at first a wider range. As Aristotle, observed, at first children call all men Daddy and all women Mommy. A 'daddy' is a type, not narrowly the paternal parent. Our knowledge begins in confusion, with generalities that must be progressively specified. And so it is with moral knowledge.

Consider the development of the *Nicomachean Ethics*. In the first book, Aristotle establishes that there is an ultimate end of human activity and goes on to identify the marks of the ultimate end. The end is the good in the strong sense of the word and pursuit of the good will make us good. Virtue is that which makes the one having it good and renders his action good. Virtue or excellence in the pursuit of the good – that is the aim. Virtue is a modality, an adverbial modification of action: its *eu*, its being well done. To do a thing well is to do it virtuously. The human thing, what sets us off, is rational activity. That can only mean that the excellence or virtue of rational activity will make us and our actions good.

Alas, rational activity is a polysemous phrase; there is rational activity and there is rational activity. Very well, then there is a plurality of virtues involved in the ultimate end. The remainder of the *Ethics* explores those different senses of virtue, first moral virtue, then intellectual virtues, the virtues of practical intellect first and then of speculative intellect. The work culminates with the recognition that only contemplation satisfies the definition of ultimate end in a fully adequate way. And the chief concern of contemplation is the divine.

Once more, we seem to have an argument against the basic role of theism in ethics. It seems to show up only at the end.

The very way that moral precepts are ranked conveys this procedure – *communissima, communia, propria*. That suggests that the first, most common precepts are confused and general and await specification. Are they thereby somehow unsure? Consider the analogy of our knowledge of the natural world. It is at the outset of the *Physics* that we are reminded that our knowledge of nature begins with confused generalities and proceeds towards ever more specific knowledge of the things that have come to be as the result of change. It is in virtue of our first grasp of such things that we discern the three elements of any change – matter, form and privation – and the minimal constituents of any product of change – matter and form. The fact that this analysis covers every change does not make it less sure. But it whets our desire for more specific knowledge. Specific knowledge is not the result of deduction, as if genera contained the differences that divide them into species. Only by way of more and more experience will our knowledge of the world grow more perfect. For all that, specific knowledge is implicit in the knowledge with which we begin.

Such considerations as these indicate what is meant by saying that ethics without theism is essentially inadequate. Awareness of God is implicit at the very outset of the moral life, in the desire for happiness; reflection and experience produce accounts of morality and such accounts require acknowledgment of the existence of God if they are to be adequate. That this is not just a pious plea is clear from those who have sought to provide an account of ethics without God.

If, in Jean-Paul Sartre's phrase, existence precedes essence when God has been ejected from ethics, the result is a freedom which creates its own criteria of choice. Antecedent to choice nothing is good or bad in itself. Any effort to introduce some diminution of our freedom – genetics, upbringing, whatever – is *mauvais foi*, self deception. In the theistic alternative to this, essence precedes existence. That is, we have a nature, we are creatures whose good is the fulfilment of what they are. No adequate account of who we are and what we are meant to be can be given without appeal to God. Without Him there is the chaos of relativism and the Will to Power.

Of course when Nietzsche says that God is dead he is thinking of the God of Christendom and of the faith that gave substance to western culture. So too Sartre is opposing not just theism but Christianity. It goes without saying that moral theology without God would be impossible. But theology presupposes philosophy and the rudimentary considerations I have been engaged in here are not without importance for the theologian.

Ralph McInerny
University of Notre Dame

# INTRODUCTION

The story of Aristotelianism's revival in recent academic moral philosophy is well-known. In a much simplified version: by the middle of the 20th Century, substantive ethical theory was dominated by versions of utilitarianism and Kantianism. Attention was paid to consequences, rules, intentions, obligations, and rights. Philosophers sought principles that would guide action and solve dilemmas – or they sought analysis, sometimes of a psychologically deflationary sort, of the meaning of such moral terminology. Thus consequentialist and deontological approaches competed against each other, and against positions which (in concert with larger cultural influences) called into question the very possibility of objective moral reasoning.

In this landscape, the philosophical concerns central to an Aristotelian approach – virtue, happiness, contemplation, the *summum bonum* – were largely absent, and were introduced, if at all, only as historical curiosities. Then, thanks to a number of perceptive authors influenced by Aristotle and Aquinas, together with analytic philosophy's increasing interest in issues of practical reasoning and the notion of virtue, the Aristotelian tradition was re-introduced and steadily gained authority as at least a viable alternative moral philosophy.

But a funny thing happened on the way back to Aristotle. As the now common "virtue ethics" label implies, focus was on the concept of habits of perfection, with comparatively little attention paid to the metaphysical framework in which Aristotle himself described them. Especially missing has been the notion that virtue orients the moral agent to God.

Take two prominent thinkers in the virtue revival. Elizabeth Anscombe, to whom the contemporary Aristotelian turn is usually traced, actually presented virtue as an alternative to more intrinsically theological ethical concepts: moral law implies a lawgiver, but virtue, Anscombe implied, does not. Likewise Alasdair MacIntyre, whose *After Virtue* was a landmark text in the virtue theory revival, drew on almost every intellectual resource available, including political and social theory, literary criticism, history and psychology, even postmodern attention to narrative – but not traditional metaphysics.

Indeed, the persuasiveness of Anscombe and the brilliance of MacIntyre can be partly traced to their ability to present Aristotelian moral thought independently of its metaphysical and theological context. The contemporary neglect of the role of the divine in Aristotelian moral philosophy should perhaps be understood as a part of an understandable concession to the contemporary rhetorical situation. But it cannot long be ignored that from an Aristotelian perspective, moral reflection had an inevitably theological orientation. For Aristotle and Aquinas, God was both object and model of contemplation, the highest form of life; God is the author or designer of the human natures that virtue perfects; Aristotle even asks, as serious questions, whether happiness comes from God, and whether it is possible to be friends with God.

The role of these questions in the interpretation of Aristotle and Aquinas, and their continuing relevance to contemporary moral thought, are the concerns of the authors brought together in this volume.

The first three essays consider the relationship of Aristotle and Aquinas. Kevin Flannery explores the possibility of "friendship with God" within the Aristotelian framework. Flannery offers close readings of relevant passages from Aristotle and Aquinas to illuminate the difference between Aristotle's philosophical conception of friendship and the conception made possible by Christian faith. Christopher Kaczor's contribution takes up the vexed question of the significance of Aquinas's Christian faith for his status as an Aristotelian. Starting with the question of whether or in what sense it is possible to be good without God, Kaczor offers a reading of Aquinas's *Sententia libri ethicorum*, arguing that Aquinas retains a notion of what it is to be a good human being such that it is not dependent on belief in God. Thus he finds in Aquinas a theoretical framework that is properly philosophical and continuous with Aristotle's. Antonio Donato reaches a somewhat different conclusion by considering the question of contemplation. He argues that when Aquinas finds the notion of Christian beatitude latent in Aristotle's qualifications about contemplation, this is not an innocent discovery but a deliberately creative theological transformation. But Aquinas's departure from Aristotle is not necessarily dependent on Christian faith, for Donato finds precedent for the distinction between perfect and imperfect contemplation in the Neoplatonic tradition.

The next three essays consider the metaphysical presuppositions of Thomistic moral philosophy. Anthony J. Lisska draws on discussions within contemporary analytic philosophy to defend the naturalism of Aquinas's ethics. Articulating the notion of substantial form in a natural kind ontology, he shows how it plays a role in Aquinas's ethics, and argues that in its general form it need not make specifically theological appeals. Fulvio Di Blasi raises a question similar to Kaczor's – in what sense is knowledge of God necessary in the moral life? – but explores it through the metaphysics of participation and the convertibility of being and goodness. His project thus becomes an exploration of what means for a rational creature to share in divine perfection. Giacomo Samek Lodovici likewise considers the metaphysical psychology underlying Thomas's ethics. His reflections on the nature of the person and its inclinations lead to a

conclusion that reinforce's Di Blasi's: that the quest for happiness cannot be satisfied short of knowledge and love of God.

The last three essays consider the notion of law and the teleological view of
nature. Robert Gahl addresses the concept of authority in law and challenges the
notion of a purely naturalistic ethics in Aquinas. The fundamental question, for
Aquinas, is not whether one can know the natural law apart from God, but how
much the Christian understanding of God through faith changes what we understand about how the natural law can be fulfilled: given our status as fallen
beings, even our fulfillment of the natural law is radically dependent on grace.
Marie George defends Aristotle's teleological view against Neo-Darwinian
philosophers. As far as human nature is concerned, the advantages of Aristotle's
account come from three main theses, namely (1) that reason is an immaterial
faculty, (2) that "we are truly free," and (3) that our nature "is fundamentally
unchanging." As George argues, finality in nature leads to the question of God's
existence, which, in turn, affects our attitude towards nature and ethics.   Finally,
Daniel McInerny responds to challenges from "new natural law" theorists about
the incommensurablity of human goods. McInerny allows that for Aquinas
human goods are heterogenous but they are hierarchically ordered, and the
notion of a hierarchy among goods is directly relevant to finality and human
choice.

# Can an Aristotelian Consider Himself a Friend of God?[1]

## Kevin L. Flannery, S.J.

Usually when, as here, a paper's title is a question, one learns the answer only some way into the argument. Ralph McInerny will probably tell you that that is a good way to write – or, at least, to write a mystery story. But I am going to violate that canon of good writing by telling you the answer to the question right away. It is no. An Aristotelian – by which I mean a man who holds consistently to the ideas of the Philosopher without going beyond them – cannot consider himself a friend of God.

There is a well-known reason for maintaining this. An Aristotelian cannot claim to be a friend of God since Aristotle holds that friendship requires equality and there is no equality between God and man. Let me offer some items of proof. In *Nicomachean Ethics* [*EN*] viii,7, for instance, having just said that in friendship quantitative parity is essential, Aristotle remarks:

> This becomes clear if there is a great interval in respect of excellence or vice or wealth or anything else between the parties; for then they are no longer friends, and do not even expect to be so. And this is most manifest in the case of the gods; for they surpass us most decisively in all good things.[2]

Aristotle goes on to say similar things about the possibility of friendship

---

1   I have discussed some of the things discussed here in an article, in Italian, with a similar title: see K.L. Flannery, "Può un aristotelico considerarsi amico di Dio?" in *Domanda sul Bene e Domanda su Dio*, ed. L. Melina and J. Noriega (Rome: Pontificia Università Lateranense / MURSIA, 1999), pp. 131–37. I thank for their comments on the present paper Frs. Stephen Brock and Robert Gahl. I thank Dr. Fulvio Di Blasi for his kindness in inviting me to the Notre Dame conference "Ethics Without God?" and for his remarks after the paper.

2   *EN* viii,7,1158b33–36. For Aristotelian translations in this paper, I make use of J. Barnes, ed. *The Complete Works of Aristotle: The Revised Oxford Translation* (Princeton: Princeton University Press, 1984) – sometimes, however, altering a translation without further mention.

between ordinary folk and kings or those who excel in virtue or wisdom. And then he remarks:

> In such cases it is not possible to define exactly up to what point friends can remain friends; for much can be taken away and friendship remain, but when one party is removed to a great distance, as God is, the possibility of friendship ceases. This is in fact the origin of the question whether friends really wish for their friends the greatest goods, e.g. that of being gods; since in that case their friends will no longer be friends to them, and therefore will not be good things for them (for friends *are* good things) [1159a5-8].

For the moment, I do not want to discuss the issue of men becoming gods; it is enough right now to have established that, as rational beings becomes more divine, they become less capable of friendship with mere men.

Another item of proof comes in the *Magna Moralia*, book two, chapter eleven, where a student of Aristotle's records the thought of the Master:

> First, then, we must determine what kind of friendship we are in search of. For, there is, people think, a friendship [φιλία] towards gods and toward things without life, but here they are wrong. For friendship, we maintain, exists only where there can be an exchange of affection, but friendship towards God does not admit of love being returned, nor at all of loving. For it would be strange if one were to say that one loved Zeus [*MM* ii,11,1208b26-31].[3]

There are passages in Aristotle where he says that friendship between man and God (or the gods) *is* possible. In *EN* viii,12, for instance, he says, "The friendship of children to parents, and of men to gods, is a relation to them as to something good and superior."[4] And in *EE* vii,10, he says, "the friendship of man and wife is a friendship based on utility, a partnership; that of father and son is the same of that of God to man, of the benefactor to the benefited, and in general of the natural ruler to the natural subject."[5] Note that by combining these two passages we discover a two way relationship of friendship: of men toward the gods (πρὸς θεούς) and of God towards man (πρὸς ἄνθρωπον).

---

3    On the authenticity of *MM*, see J.M. Cooper, "The *Magna Moralia* and Aristotle's moral philosophy," *American Journal of Philology* 94 (1973): 327–49, and K.L. Flannery, "The Aristotelian first principle of practical reason," *The Thomist* 59 (1995): 441–64, esp. p. 450, n.14.

4    ἔστι δ᾽ ἡ μὲν πρὸς γονεῖς φιλία τέκνοις, καὶ ἀνθρώποις πρὸς θεους, ὡς πρὸς ἀγαθὸν καὶ ὑπερέχον [*EN* viii,12,1162a4–5; my emphasis]. See also *EN* viii,10,1160b25–26.

5    γυναικὸς δὲ καὶ ἀνδρὸς φιλία ὡς χρήσιμον καὶ κοινωνία· πατρὸς δὲ καὶ υἱοῦ ἡ αὐτὴ ἥπερ θεοῦ πρὸς ἄνθρωπον καὶ τοῦ εὖ ποιήσαντος πρὸς τὸν παθόντα καὶ ὅλως τοῦ φύσει ἄρχοντος πρὸς τὸν φύσει ἀρχόμενον [*EE* vii,10,1242a31–35].

Such passages as these in which Aristotle speaks of friendship with God are, however, easily accounted for. They point not to a contradiction within the theory but rather (as one comes to expect in reading Aristotle) to a multiplicity of senses of the word 'friendship' (φιλία). There is, of course, the well-known three-part division of friendship into the friendship of virtue, the friendship of pleasure, and the friendship of utility. But Aristotle also says, in the *Eudemian Ethics*, that these three types are themselves found in two, more fundamental categories of friendship: friendship according to equality [φιλία κατὰ τὸ ἴσον] and friendship according to preeminence [φιλία καθ' ὑπεροχήν].[6] So, there are at least six types of friendship.[7] When Aristotle says that friendship between man and God is possible, he obviously has in mind a type of friendship different from that which he denies of them. Which type is this? That is, which type (or types) of friendship is impossible between man and God? The passage cited initially above, from *EN* viii,7, strongly suggest that it is any type of friendship according to equality. In that passage Aristotle speaks of God (or the gods) as standing at "a great interval" or "a great distance" from man, saying that this is what makes friendship impossible.

## II

This idea that there is a great distance between God and man ought not to present difficulties for Christian readers of Aristotle – or whom we might dare to call "Christian Aristotelians," such as the author of *Shakespearean Variations*, if I might employ a definite description in order to protect said individual from too easy mockery and disdain. For although we find in the Gospel of John, for instance, many scriptural passages that suggest that one can become a friend of God through union with Christ, it is still very important in the Christian Faith to maintain that, in another sense, friendship with God is quite impossible. If there were no such separation between God and man, the Incarnation, in which God *becomes* man, would be nothing to marvel at. If there were no such separation between God and the human sphere, two millennia of liturgical worship would have been a huge mistake: we ought long ago to have banned incense and kneeling and the striking of breasts, in favor of the standard rite of American Jesuit theologates: the coffee table Mass.

In Thomas Aquinas's *Quaestio Disputata de Caritate*, we find at one point the following objection to Thomas's position that charity, which establishes a strict connection between God and man,[8] is a virtue:

---

6    *EE* vii,4,1239a1–4.

7    Aristotle recognizes also a distinction between "moral friendship" and "legal friendship" [*EE* vii,10,1243a2–14; see also *EN* viii,13,1162b21–1163a1].

8    See *Quaestio Disputata de Caritate* q. 1, a. 1 ad 4, ad 8, and ad 16.

According to the Philosopher in book eight of the *Ethics*,[9] friendship consists in a certain equality. But the inequality of God with respect to us is of
the highest degree, as of something infinitely distant. There cannot, therefore, be friendship on God's part with respect to us, or on our part with
respect to God; and so charity, which designates such friendship, does not
appear to be a virtue.[10]

The objection is obviously addressing the issue that concerns us at the
moment: i.e., whether the distance between God and man posited by Aristotle
excludes the possibility of friendship. There were a number of routes that
Thomas might have taken in order to escape this conclusion (and the further
conclusion that, therefore, divine charity is no human virtue): he might, for
instance, have pointed to passages in the same book of the *Nicomachean Ethics*
in which Aristotle discusses other types of friendship that do not require strict
equality.[11] But he took no such route. His reply is rather that:

> ...charity is not of man in as much as he is man but in as much as, through
> the participation of grace, he becomes God [*fit Deus* (!)] and a son of God,
> in accordance with the first letter of St. John (chapter three, verse one),
> "See what love [*caritatem*] the Father has given to us: that we should be
> called sons of God and be so."[12]

In other words, were it not for Christ and the grace of the Incarnation, we would
indeed be in the situation described by Aristotle: with a God infinitely beyond
our ken and to be feared and honored rather than talked to as if to a friend. Or
better: were it not for Christ, we would be left *only* with a God to be feared and

---

9    The reference appears to be to *EN* viii,6,1158b1; see also 13,1162a34–36.

10   *Quaestio Disputata de Caritate* q.un. a.2 obj.15: "Praeterea, secundum
     Philosophum in VIII *Ethic.*, amicitia in quadam aequalitate consistit. Sed Dei ad nos
     est maxima inaequalitas, sicut infinite distantium. Ergo non potest esse amicitia Dei
     ad nos, vel nostri ad Deum; et ita caritas, quae huiusmodi amicitiam designat, non
     videtur esse virtus."

11   Although they do require *some* form of equality: see *EN* viii,13,1162a34–b4.

12   *Quaestio Disputata de Caritate* q.un. a.2 ad 15: "Ad decimumquintum dicendum,
     quod caritas non est virtus hominis in quantum est homo, sed in quantum per par-
     ticipationem gratiae fit Deus et filius Dei, secundum illud I Ioan. III, 1: videte
     qualem caritatem dedit nobis Pater, ut filii Dei nominemur et simus." See also
     Thomas's *ST* I-II q.109 a.3 ad 1 ("quandam societatem spiritualem cum Deo");
     q.110 a.1 ("Alia autem dilectio [Dei ad creaturam] est specialis, secundum quam
     trahit creaturam rationalem supra conditionem naturae, ad participationem divini
     boni. Et secundum hanc dilectionem dicitur aliquem diligere simpliciter, quia
     secundum hanc dilectionem vult Deus simpliciter creaturae bonum aeternum, quod
     est ipse"); q.110 a.3; q.112 a.1; II-II q.23 a.1; q.24 a.2. I thank Fr. Stephen Brock
     for these references.

honored, and without the salvation that cannot be conceived otherwise than in the light of the Incarnation, whereby we become one with God in our union with the Son of Mary, who was also the Son of God. As it is, our situation is one which continues to demand our natural awe and reverence for God, but acknowledges also that in Christ we are on such intimate terms with God that we can address him as our Father or even – in Christ – as our friend: "I no longer call you servants, for a servant does not know what his master does. I have called you rather friends [φίλους], for everything that I have heard from my Father I have made known to you" [John 15.15]. The Incarnation does not nullify our obligation to worship and to honor God: it just assures us that it has been – and will be – made complete, in a way undreamed of by human reason alone.

But it is one of the extraordinary things about Aristotle that he so often sets out the framework in which the unimaginable can be made intelligible, in a precise manner. There is no doubt that Aristotle holds that God has no friends. At one point in the *Eudemian Ethics*, he asks whether it can be true that "if a man be in all respects self-sufficient [αὐτάρχης], he will have a friend: whether a friend is sought from want or not? Or is the good man perfectly self-sufficient?" [1244b2-4].[13] And a couple of lines later he applies this idea to God: "This is most apparent with respect to God," he says: "for it is clear that, needing nothing, neither will he have need of a friend, nor will he ever *have* that of which he has no need."[14] And yet, as we have already seen, he maintains in the same work that there *is* friendship between God and his creations, i.e., friendship according to preeminence.

These two strands of thought are reconciled by simply acknowledging that friendship is one thing, being friends quite another. Aristotle says this in as many words at the beginning *Eudemian Ethics* book seven, chapter four. With reference to friendship according to equality and friendship according to preeminence, he remarks: "Both are friendships; those who are *friends*, however, are friends according to equality."[15] In other words, there can be φιλία where there are no φίλοι. In the *Nicomachean Ethics*, in speaking about another type of friendship according to preeminence, i.e., that pertaining to kings, Aristotle remarks: "The friendship between a king and his subjects depends on an excess of benefits conferred [ἐν ὑπεροχῇ εὐεργεσίας]; for he confers benefits on his

---

13  ἀπορήσειε γὰρ ἄν τις πότερον, εἴ τις εἴη κατὰ πάντα αὐτάρκης, ἔσται τούτῳ <...> φίλος. εἰ κατ᾽ ἔνδειαν ζητεῖται φίλος, ἢ οὔ; ἢ ἔσται <ὁ> ἀγαθὸς αὐταρκέστατος [*EE* vii,12,1244b2–5: R. Walzer and J. Mingay, *Aristotelis: Ethica Eudemia*, Oxford Classical Texts (Oxford: Clarendon, 1991).]

14  μάλιστα δὲ τοῦτο φανερὸν ἐπὶ θεοῦ· δῆλον γὰρ ὡς οὐδενὸς προσδεόμενος οὐδὲ φίλου δεήσεται, οὐδ᾽ ἔσται αὐτῷ οὗ γε μηδ᾽ ἐνδεής ποτε [*EE* vii,12,1244b7–10: Walzer, et al. 1991].

15  φιλίαι μὲν οὖν ἀμφότεραι, φίλοι δ᾽ οἱ κατὰ τὴν ἰσότητα [*EE* vii,4,1239a4–5; my emphasis].

subjects if, being good, he cares for them with a view to their well-being, as a shepherd does for his sheep" [*EN* viii,11,1161a11-14]. There can indeed exist a certain friendship between a shepherd and his sheep. But this does not mean that the friends of the shepherd are sheep – or *can* be sheep. Similarly with God: the benefits he bestows – life, happiness, knowledge – establish a certain relationship of friendship. But this does not make God and us friends: "buddies." Nor does this (i.e., that he is not our friend) derogate from his goodness. As Aristotle says in the passage we have just seen, it is *because* of his goodness that this type of friendship exists.

This is the theoretical framework into which Christianity inserts itself: a framework in which there is a distinction between being related to God as awestruck subject and being related to him as his friend. The utterly surprising completion of the framework is provided by Jesus Christ, who makes it possible that we be both at once. The framework itself, however – the basic setting of the story – had already been set out clearly by Aristotle.

### III

Actually, however, this is all still a bit simplistic – that is, this idea that these two types of friendship with God are to be isolated the one from the other: on the one hand, Aristotelian friendship according to preeminence, wherein God remains at an unapproachable distance, and, on the other, Christian friendship according to equality, wherein we become friends of God by being one with Christ who is one with the Father. Do not get me wrong: the two *are* distinct; and therefore the Aristotelian scheme is no less impressive than I have been suggesting – not to mention the tying together of the scheme in Christ. But our understanding especially of Aristotelian friendship with God according to preeminence requires yet some work.

For one thing, if we were to say simply that according to Aristotle "God remains at an unapproachable distance," this would play into the hands of those who maintain that the God of Aristotle is a solipsistic one, with no interest in the doings of men and, consequently, no knowing effect on those doings. We all know the text that best supports such an interpretation, i.e., the passage in the twelfth book of the *Metaphysics* where God is defined as thinking on thinking (νόησις νοήσεως: *Metaph.* xii,9,1074b3) whose only worthy object of thought is himself. But there are precious few texts that point in this direction and plenty of others that point in the direction of a God who is not only interested in what happens here but can also have an effect upon it.

Take, for instance, the remark in *Nicomachean Ethics* x,8, where he uses as the basis of an argument that philosophical contemplation is the highest vocation the idea that the gods are concerned about human affairs (1179a24-9):

> For if the gods [he says] have any care for human affairs, as it seems they

do [ὥσπερ δοκεῖ], it would be reasonable both that they should delight in that which was best and most akin to them (i.e., intellect) and that they should reward those who love and honor this most, as caring for the things that are dear to them and acting both rightly and nobly.

And in the *Eudemian Ethics* Aristotle says the exchange of roles that occurs in the city – a citizen becomes alternatively commander and commanded – is done not out of benevolence "in the way that God acts benevolently"[16] but for utilitarian reasons. Both these passages suggest – or, to be more precise, they *say* – that God (or the gods) pays (pay) attention to what happens in the world of men.

Let me offer some more items of proof. In *Metaphysics*, book twelve, chapter nine, in the very sentence in which Aristotle uses the phrase νόησις νοήσεως and rejects the notion that God might have as his proper object something other than himself, he tells us why this is important: it is important since otherwise God's power would be diminished. "He [God], therefore, thinks himself, since he is the most powerful [τὸ κράτιστον]: that is, his thinking is thinking on thinking."[17] But the power Aristotle is determined to preserve is very clearly the power whereby God has an effect in the world. This is apparent from chapter six of the same book and his criticism of the Platonists. The problem with the Forms, he says, is that they *do* nothing: they have no effects.[18] What follows this remark, in book twelve, chapters seven through ten (which include the remark about νόησις νοήσεως and "the most powerful"), is put forward as an *alternative* to Platonic theory: an alternative in which effective power *is* present.

That God's seemingly inward-looking characteristics are precisely what drive his external effects is made clear in *Physics* viii,5. There Aristotle speaks approvingly of Anaxagoras, according to whom "Mind" (or God) is "impassive and unmixed" – that is to say, unmixed with the world. This does not make Mind less influential but more. Says Aristotle by way of interpretation of Anaxagoras, Mind "would only cause motion the way it does being unmoved, and it would only *assert its power* [κρατοίη] being unmixed."[19] So, the unmoved mover's separate status as contemplator of himself is precisely for the purpose of having an effect outside himself.

That God's efficaciousness is not an unknowing one becomes apparent in

---

16   ἔστι δὲ ἐνταῦθα καὶ ἄρχον καὶ ἀρχόμενον οὔτε τὸ φυσικὸν οὔτε τὸ βασιλικόν, ἀλλὰ τὸ ἐν τῷ μέρει, οὐδὲ τούτου ἕνεκα ὅπως εὖ ποιῇ ὁ θεός, ἀλλ᾽ ἵνα ἴσον ᾖ τοῦ ἀγαθοῦ καὶ τῆς λειτουργίας. *EE* vii,10,1242b27–30: F. Susemihl, ed. *(Aristotelis: Ethica Eudemia) Eudemi Rhodii Ethica* (Teubner: Leipzig, 1884).]

17   αὐτὸν ἄρα νοεῖ, εἴπερ ἐστὶ τὸ κράτιστον, καὶ ἔστιν ἡ νόησις νοήσεως νόησις [*Metaph.* xii,9,1074b34].

18   *Metaph.* xii,6,1071b12–32.

19   διὸ καὶ Ἀναξαγόρας ὀρθῶς λέγει, τὸν νοῦν ἀπαθῆ φάσκων καὶ ἀμιγῆ εἶναι, ἐπειδή γε κινήσεως ἀρχὴν αὐτὸν εἶναι ποιεῖ· οὕτω γὰρ μόνως ἂν κινοίη ἀκίνητος ὢν καὶ κρατοίη ἀμιγὴς ὤν [*Phys.* viii,5,256b24–27].

some often neglected remarks in book one, chapter two, of the *Metaphysics*. Aristotle says there that the knowledge most suited to God is "divine knowledge" (or divine science). This knowledge is not unlike that which he goes on to attribute to the first unmoved mover in book twelve: it is the most noble type of knowledge since it is both knowledge that God *has* and it *has* God as its object. But it is also knowledge in which humans can share, for, as he says, "divine power cannot be jealous" [*Metaph.* i,2,983a2-3]. It is knowledge that extends to the present realm: it is, in short, metaphysics.[20] God therefore knows metaphysics – and not just the metaphysics of the twelfth book of (his work) the *Metaphysics*.

So then, we have a remark in Aristotle, according to which God has as his thought's object himself as thinking on thinking; we have also various other remarks, some of them quite close to the remark about thinking on thinking, which suggest that God is not closed in upon himself but has power, infused with knowledge, in the world known also to us. One way of accounting for these separate strands of thought is to say that Aristotle was simply inconsistent – or, perhaps more plausibly, inconsistent over time, holding, at one point in his career, traditional ideas about the relationship of God (or the gods) to the world of men, at another time propounding a more philosophically sophisticated theory which isolates God from that world. I prefer rather the solution proposed by Thomas Aquinas: that, in thinking on himself, God knows – and controls – all other things.[21] This saves us from having to do, almost literally, a "hatchet-job" on Aristotle, positing separate developmental strata in his writings: sometimes within individual books, sometimes even within a single sentence.

## IV

Let us look now at the other vector in the God-man relationship. That is, I have been arguing that even within the Aristotelian theory of friendship, in which the friendship of friends is distinct from friendship according to preeminence (καθ' ὑπεροχὴν), the latter, of which friendship between God and men is an instance, does not entail a lack of interest of one pole for its opposite. So far I have considered only God's interest in the world, including the world of men. But what

---

20  This most universal type of knowledge embraces all subordinate knowledge: *Metaph.* i,2,982a23, 982b2–4. See also *Metaph.* iii,4,1000b3–6, where the theory of Empedocles is criticized because it makes of God, who is prevented by his nature from knowing all the elements, "less wise than all others."

21  *in Metaph.* §2614: "Considerandum est autem quod Philosophus intendit ostendere, quod Deus non intelligit aliud, sed seipsum, inquantum intellectum est perfectio intelligentis, et eius, quod est intelligere. Manifestum est autem quod nihil aliud sic potest intelligi a Deo, quod sit perfectio intellectus eius. Nec tamen sequitur quod omnia alia a se sint ei ignota; nam intelligendo se, intelligit omnia alia."

can we say about man's response to God? Even granting (for the sake of not going beyond Aristotle) that man cannot be a *friend* of God, is man's task simply to acknowledge the unbridgeable distance between himself and the divine and to set about being more human, or is he not called rather to become like God as much as possible?

We are dealing now, of course, with the ancient concept of ὁμοίωσις θεῷ, found most famously in Plato and in Plotinus,[22] but found also, I would maintain, in Aristotle, even if that exact phrase does not appear. We have already in effect seen this in the passage from *Metaphysics*, book one, chapter two, where Aristotle says God's knowledge is the most divine type of knowledge and that, not being jealous, he shares it with his rational creatures. But Aristotle says this also most explicitly, and in an ethical context, in the tenth book of the *Nicomachean Ethics*. Having excluded the possibility that God (or the gods) might have a, strictly speaking, practical life, he says: "the activity of God [ἡ τοῦ θεοῦ ἐνέργεια], which surpasses all others in blessedness, must be contemplative; and of human activities, therefore, that which is most akin [συγγενεστάτη] to this must be most of the nature of happiness" [*EN* x,8,1178b21-3]. He then goes on to say, "To the gods, the whole life is blessed; to men, in so far as some likeness [ὁμοίωμα] of such activity belongs to them" [*EN* x,8,1178b25-7] – i.e., some likeness of the "activity of God."[23] Indeed, Aristotle directly confronts the argument that, given the vast difference between God and man, man should renounce any pretensions of becoming like God:

> If intellect is divine, then, in comparison with man, the life according to it is divine in comparison with human life. But we must not follow those who advise us, being men, to think of human things, and, being mortal, of mortal things, but must, so far as we can, make ourselves immortal, and strain every nerve to live in accordance with the best thing in us; for, even if it [i.e., the best thing in us] be small in bulk, much more does it in power and worth surpass everything.[24]

Remarks such as these force upon us an understanding of the role of the divine in Aristotelian ethics more complicated than is, perhaps, at first apparent.

---

22   φυγὴ δὲ ὁμοίωσις θεῷ κατὰ τὸ δυνατόν· ὁμοίωσις δὲ δίκαιον καὶ ὅσιον μετὰ φρονήσεως γενέσθαι [*Theaetetus* 176A9–B2]; in Plotinus, see *Enneades* I,2,1.

23   τοῖς μὲν γὰρ θεοῖς ἅπας ὁ βίος μακάριος, τοῖς δ᾽ ἀνθρώποις, ἐφ᾽ ὅσον ὁμοίωμά τι τῆς τοιαύτης ἐνεργείας ὑπάρχει. This is the key text of John Dudley's very good treatment of the role of God and contemplation in Aristotle's ethics, see p. 5 of J. Dudley, *Dio e contemplazione in Aristotele: Il fondamento metafisico dell'Etica Nicomachea* (Milan: Vita e pensiero, 1999), this being a translation of J. Dudley, *Gott und Theoria bei Aristoteles: Die metaphysische Grundlage der Nikomachischen Ethik* (Frankfurt am Main: P. Lang, 1982).

24   *EN* x,7,1177b30–1178a2; cp. *Metaph.* i,2,982b31–2.

I have to admit that in a book of my own I relegated the divine in ethics primarily to ethics' *ends*.[25] Aristotelian ethics cannot be, as, for example, Martha
Nussbaum would have it, independent of religious belief since the very goods
that help to establish its structure are described by Aristotle as divine – and even
as gods.[26] Human acts are articulated: they stretch over time. Since the gods are
simple, we cannot associate them with that which stretches over time; but we
can associate them, he says, with the ends which, standing at the extremes, are
without parts. All this I still regard as true, and I would even add a passage to
those I cited in my book: i.e., the first chapter of the second book of *De caelo*,
where Aristotle speaks of the gods of the ancients as "the limit of all other movement."[27] But this cannot be the whole of the matter since Aristotle clearly has
more in mind when he urges us to "strain every nerve to live in accordance with
the best thing in us." We do not have to strain every nerve to perform actions
that finish in ends, since they *all* finish in ends – as do, for that matter, the
actions of dogs, slugs, and even rocks, according to Aristotle.

Becoming like God and becoming better men is, according to Aristotle, a
matter of organizing our lives in accordance with truth – or, perhaps better, in
accordance with *truths*. Such organizing concerns in the first place, or at the
highest level of living well, philosophical truths about the universe: in short,
metaphysics. I have already relayed some of what Aristotle says about this "most
divine of sciences" in chapter two of the first book of the *Metaphysics*. But it is
also clear in that chapter that the study of metaphysics is continuous with the
more human and practical pursuits. Metaphysics is portrayed there not as an
activity unconnected with the ethical lives of men but as that which ultimately
gives it sense. The man who pursues knowledge in its purest form and in the
most disinterested way, says Aristotle, will pursue the knowledge found in metaphysics; but he will do this because it is knowledge of the ends that inform all
other forms of knowledge, especially practical knowledge. All desire for knowledge finishes in the desire to know "the first principles and causes," which
Aristotle identifies as "the good" [τἀγαθὸν].[28]

If, therefore, becoming better men involves becoming more like God, living well (ethics) is quite a complicated affair – as is the way in which God
comes into it (although only from our point of view, not from his). It involves
not just our orientation toward the goods (or the good) but also the way in which
we organize our personal lives, our families and other communities, in such a

---

25  See K.L. Flannery, *Acts amid Precepts: The Aristotelian Logical Structure of
     Thomas Aquinas's Moral Theory* (Washington, D.C. / Edinburgh: Catholic
     University of America Press / T & T Clark, 2001), pp. 22–23.
26  See *EN* i,12,1101b25–7; 1102a2–4; x,8,1178b7–22.
27  *Cael.* ii,1,284a5–6. See also *EN* vi,13,1145a10–11. That the extremes are involved
     in practical reasoning is apparent from *EN* vii,11,1143a36–b3.
28  *Metaph.* i,2,982b9–10. See also *Metaph.* xii,7,1072b3.

way that they and we can thrive. It involves ordering professions, such as medicine, according to rational principles, i.e., principles that truly lead to the proper ends of such professions. It involves establishing and maintaining universities in a way that respects the designs of the creator of the universe they are set up to study.

It is true that God's knowledge of all such matters is simple. It can only be so. He does not need, for instance, to call the various details to mind; he does not need to put them in order. The knowledge that he has of man's complex city is immediate and intuitive. But this does not mean that we should understand his importance for the organization of human culture as similarly simple: occupying only the "limit regions," so to speak. If what Aristotle says in *Metaphysics* book one, chapter two, is true and the knowledge that God has is the same knowledge that we might share in, and if we are encouraged to imitate it, to "strain every nerve to live in accordance with the best thing in us," then being moral is not just a matter of *aiming* at God but of intending to make our complex cultural structures correspond somehow to his simple knowledge of them. And that is a complicated task.[29]

V

To conclude, then, we have before us now the major pieces of the puzzle: i.e., the major ideas necessary for understanding the difference between a Christian conception of friendship with God and an Aristotelian one. An Aristotelian – by which, to repeat, I mean a man who holds consistently to the ideas of the Philosopher without going beyond them – cannot consider himself a *friend* of God (in the sense of a companion), although he can say that there exists between himself and God a relationship of friendship. Moreover, although God's side of the relationship must be conceived of in a special way,[30] the friendship between God and man, according to this conception, involves real interaction between the two poles of the relationship. A Christian, on the other hand, can consider himself (at least possibly) a friend – a companion – of God through union with

---

29   In the final chapter of *Metaphysics*, book twelve, Aristotle says that we must "consider also in which of two ways the nature of the universe contains the good or the highest good, whether as something separate and by itself, or as the order of the parts. Probably in both ways, as an army does. For the good is found both in the order and in the leader..." [*Metaph.* xii,10,1075a11–14].

30   See Thomas Aquinas, *ST* 1.28.1 ad 3: *[C]um creatura procedat a Deo in diversitate naturae, Deus est extra ordinem totius creaturae, nec ex eius natura est eius habitudo ad creaturas. Non enim producit creaturas ex necessitate suae naturae, sed per intellectum et per voluntatem, ut supra dictum est. Et ideo in Deo non est realis relatio ad creaturas. Sed in creaturis est realis relatio ad Deum, quia creaturae continentur sub ordine divino, et in earum natura est quod dependeant a Deo.*

Christ. In addition, the Christian is party to a friendship with God that is "according to preeminence," a relationship such as is given a precise philosophical account in Aristotle.

How, then, might we characterize in a succinct way the difference between the Aristotelian and the Christian ways of conceiving friendship with God? One is tempted to say that the difference is that only Christians hold that they can become true friends of God by becoming equal to him through union with Christ. But we have already seen that Aristotle considers at least the possibility that a man might become a god [*EN* viii,7,1159a5-12]. The second-century Peripatetic commentator Aspasius argues that becoming a god is impossible and that, therefore, Aristotle is merely considering an hypothesis.[31] I think that this is quite likely correct. When Aristotle introduces the matter, he does so as if he were considering a standard aporia: "This," he says, "is in fact the origin of the question whether friends really wish for their friends the greatest goods, e.g. that of being gods...".[32] But even if it is true that Aristotle does not think that men can become gods, still, his theory does allow for the possibility, even if it is just an hypothetical possibility. We cannot say, therefore, that he gives us no way of understanding true friendship with God. Indeed, what he says, even if hypothetically, is remarkably similar to the position of Thomas Aquinas, which we have already seen: man becomes friends with God only by becoming equal to him.[33]

What then *is* the difference between Aristotle and Christianity in this regard? The difference is that, for Aristotle, in order (hypothetically) to become a friend of God, we must cease to be men.[34] He saw no other way. Christ, on the other hand, brought us the Good News that we can be friends of God without ceasing to be men. We can do this since he, Christ, was both God and man and we can become one with him. This is information to which Aristotle had no access. It comes to us by Revelation and by grace. It makes all the difference.

---

31  διὸ καὶ ἀπορεῖται εἰ βουλήσεται ὁ φίλος τῷ φίλῳ τὰ μέγιστα ἀγαθά, οἷον θεὸν γενέσθαι. φανερὸν μὲν οὖν ὅτι τὰ ἀδύνατα οὐ βουλήσεται ὁ φρόνιμος· τοιοῦτον δὲ τὸ ἐξ ἀνθρώπου θεὸν γενέσθαι· ἀλλ᾽ ἐξ ὑποθέσεως, εἰ δυνατὸν εἴη θεὸν γενέσθαι, ἆρά γε βουλήσεται; [Aspasius, *Commentaria in Aristotelem Graeca*. Vol. 19.1, *In Ethica Nicomachea quae supersunt commentaria*. Ed. G. Heylbut (Berlin: Reimer, 1889), 178.25–29].

32  ὅθεν καὶ ἀπορεῖται, μή ποτ᾽ οὐ βούλονται οἱ φίλοι τοῖς φίλοις τὰ μέγιστα τῶν ἀγαθῶν, οἷον θεοὺς εἶναι [*EN* viii,7,1159a5–7].

33  See above at note 12.

34  There is a fragment in Cicero in which Aristotle is said to speak of man as a "mortal god": "sic hominem ad duas res, ut ait Aristoteles, ad intellegendum et ad agendum esse natum quasi mortalem deum" [Rose 1886, F 61]. But also here the implication is that the two concepts do not go together: man is *"quasi* mortalem deum."

# The Divine in Thomas's Commentary on Aristotle's Nicomachean Ethics: In What Sense Can We be Good without God?

## Christopher Kaczor

What is it meant by the question, "Can we be good without God?" The question of ethics without God is not the same as the question of ethics without revelation. Indeed, revelation, at least as interpreted in the Catholic tradition, teaches that one *can* have an ethics without direct or special revelation by God. For example, certain basic truths in the moral life, such as prohibitions against intentionally killing an innocent person, stealing, and adultery, can be understood without revelation, by natural law (Romans 1:20). Although God reveals the Ten Commandments as a mercy to human beings, whose minds are darkened by the fall, in principle these truths could be known without revelation.

### Practice and Theory of Practice

Before turning explicitly to Aquinas' commentary on the *Nicomachean Ethics*, the *Sententia Libri Ethicorum*, I would like to say a word about the distinction between acknowledging basic moral truths and a systematic exposition of moral truths; and address the role of God in each kind of knowing. Grasping basic moral truth is not the same thing as having ethical knowledge, the kind that it would be possible to gain through the study of moral theology or moral philosophy. This distinction between the basic moral truths necessary to live rightly and the theoretical account of the moral life can be illustrated by the difference between what one must know to be saved and what one must know in order to possess a satisfactory account of what is required to be saved. The intellectual awareness required for salvation is quite modest according to the moral theology of Aquinas. One must merely believe in God and in God's providence.[1] On the other hand, an adequate moral theology, that is to say, an adequate account of how God saves his people, involves the mind in the complexities addressed in the *Summa Theologiae* – e.g., the relationship of faith and reason, nature and

---

1    Thomas Aquinas, *Summa Theologiae* (hereafter ST), II-II, q. 2, a. 8 ad 1.

grace, Old Law and New Law, virtues acquired and virtues infused, gifts of the Holy Spirit and fruits of the Holy Spirit, Sacraments and states in life, etc. In other words, we can distinguish between moral theology considered as a science, which requires extensive knowledge of many things, and what an individual person would actually need to know in order to be saved, which makes very modest intellectual demands.

In addressing what is necessary for salvation, Aquinas is speaking of perfect happiness, the happiness that is to be had in the next life; not imperfect happiness, that happiness that is to be had in this life by human effort. Presumably, what is necessary to achieve only imperfect happiness in this life (the subject of moral philosophy) would be even less demanding in terms of belief in the divine. And it is this form of happiness, imperfect happiness, which Aquinas explores in his commentary on Aristotle's *Nicomachean Ethics*.

For Aristotle, happiness in the present life involves (among other things) abstaining from morally wrong action. While contemplating the divine may be true happiness, one might have correct judgment that murder or adultery is wrong without having this view grounded in beliefs about God. Perhaps, one believes such truths because of the instruction of trusted parents or teachers. Or perhaps one holds the judgment because of an unreflective assumption that whatever most people believe is true should be believed. Presumably, at least for some of us, our first instruction in right or wrong came well before our first instruction in theology. We may have heard a loud voice reprimand, "Don't pull mommy's hair!" before we heard a quiet voice guide, "Our Father, who art in heaven." It would seem then that right judgment about what is to be done does not require belief in God.

But the discussion at hand, ethics without God, is not about what Aquinas calls *synesis,* a habit of judgment in realistic, individual cases, which is an almost purely practical knowledge for right living.[2] This sort of knowledge is distinguished from reason in action (prudence) simply because the final judgment about what is to be done differs from executing the actual judgment. Ethics is a practical knowledge, but of a more theoretical nature; yet, at the same time, ethics is not wholly a theoretical knowledge either. It is also knowledge of an operable object – how human actions are to be ordered rightly. This operable object is, in ethics, considered theoretically and not for immediate execution in action. In moral philosophy, we seek a theory of practice. Ethical knowledge, as developed in moral philosophy, is not immediately in the process of being

---

2    See Thomas Aquinas, *In Decem Libros Ethicorum Aristotelis ad Nicomachum Expositio,* ed. R. M. Spiazzi, O.P. (Turin: Marietti, 1964), Book 6, lect. 9 (Spiazzi numbers 1235–1256), abbreviated citation form *In Decem Libros Ethicorum Aristotelis* 6.9.1235–1256. Throughout the Latin passages come from the version of the *Sententia* found in the *Index Thomisticus,* the English translation is by C. I. Litzinger.

enacted. There is therefore a gap between a right *theory* of practice and right *practice* itself. Although moral philosophy is undertaken to direct action, it is nevertheless possible to have both right judgment about what to do here and now (*synesis*) and also correct, purely practical ethical knowledge (*prudentia*) yet lack a theory of practice. Conversely, one can have a right theory of practice but lack right purely, practical knowledge – as the person with weakness of will makes evident. A saint can flunk a course in moral philosophy just as a professor of moral philosophy can fail to act saintly.

It seems evident that one could have *synesis* without knowledge of God, for in a good society almost everyone would instinctively know the wrongfulness of certain kinds of activity, independently of divine instruction, rigorous philosophical education, or faith in God. Thus I understand the question of "ethics without God" to be asking instead: Is it possible to have moral philosophy, a theoretical account of imperfect happiness in this life, without relying on God's existence to "make good" or ultimately justify the claims made on behalf of ethics?

### The *Commentary on the Ethics*: A Work of Christian Moral Thought?

In one sense it is absolutely impossible to have an ethics without God. If God is the necessary cause of all things, then one could not have anything whatsoever without God, including water, turtles, the sun, and even the judgments of human beings about human actions. However, this point concerns the order of being and not the order of knowing. In the order of knowing, Aquinas follows Aristotle in holding that we can know things without first knowing God. God is not the first thing known by which other things are known. For human beings, the first things known are those known through the senses, and God, as an immaterial Being, cannot be known directly through the senses. What we mean to ask when we address the topic of ethics without God is, "Do we need a *Gottesbegriff* – a conception of God – in order to come to right conclusions in a theory of ethics?" In other words, does knowledge of the ethical truth depend upon or is such knowledge logically posterior to knowledge of God?

To narrow the question more, one could ask: could one have a non-theistic, Thomistic ethics? Some authors have attempted to assemble a non-theological ethic from Aquinas's *Summa Theologiae*. Wolfgang Kluxen in his *Philosophische Ethik bei Thomas von Aquin*, and John Finnis in his *Aquinas: Moral, Political, and Legal Theory* present a conception of ethics which does not presuppose theology, though it is open to a belief in God. However, it must be said that such reconstructions drawn from the *Summa Theologiae* must ignore a vast majority of the very work under consideration. Thomistic ethics as presented in the *Summa* says much more about grace than natural law, speaks at much greater length about the gifts of the Holy Spirit than about double effect, and the entire beginning of the *Secunda Secundae* is devoted to virtues which have no natural counterpart – namely, infused faith, hope, and charity. While there may be good reasons to articulate the ethics of the *Summa* with special emphasis, creative reformulation, and the intentional suppression of certain themes, such reconstructions of necessity do not tell the whole story – since the whole story for Aquinas is deeply and inescapably theological.

What is the character of this theological dimension? In fact, Aquinas' account of perfect happiness is inescapably linked, not so much with the mysteries of faith, as with the preambles of faith. In other words, it is inherently theistic, although not inherently based on special revelation.[3] If this is so, then in entertaining the possibility of a "non-theological" Thomistic ethics it might be more fruitful if we turned primarily to the *Sententia libri ethicorum*, rather than either of the two *Summae*.

Two logical obstacles immediately block this approach. The first is that the *Sententia Libri Ethicorum* is sometimes said to be merely a commentary. If the *Sententia Libri Ethicorum* is but the preparatory notes to writing the *Summa* and/or simply Aquinas' reading of the *Ethics*, then of course to interpret this commentary as expressing Aquinas' views on various matters would be deeply mistaken. Without fully retracing the arguments discussed elsewhere, I believe this view is not very plausible.[4]

Another obstacle would be the view that this commentary is itself a theological and not a philosophical work. Famously, Harry Jaffa impugned the reliability of Thomas Aquinas's *Sententia Libri Ethicorum* by saying that the commentary imported "six principles of Christian ethics," foreign to Aristotle, into the interpretation of the *Nicomachean Ethics*.[5] If the *Commentary on the Ethics* is itself a work of Christian moral thought, then the search for a non-theistic ethics cannot begin there.

By a cursory inspection alone, it is quite implausible to hold that the *Sententia Libri Ethicorum* is a book of *Christian* ethics, since the commentary makes no mention of the Trinity, the death and resurrection of Christ, or the sacraments. Just as noteworthy, the *Sententia Libri Ethicorum* does not invoke explicitly either the Old or the New Testament. Nothing is said about the Beatitudes, the parables of Jesus, or the exhortations of St. Paul. Indeed, it is hard to imagine an account of *Christian* ethics in which the name Jesus Christ does not appear a single time.

---

3    *ST*, II-II, q. 2, a. 8 ad 1.
4    See C. Kaczor, "Thomas Aquinas's *Commentary on the Ethics*: Merely an Interpretation of Aristotle?," in the *American Catholic Philosophical Quarterly* vol.78, no. 3.
5    Harry Jaffa, *Thomism and Aristotelianism: A Study of the Commentary by Thomas Aquinas on the Nicomachean Ethics* (Chicago: University of Chicago Press, 1952).

Jaffa's complaint might be more accurately described as a protest against Aquinas' *theological* beliefs slipped into this philosophical commentary, namely: belief in divine providence; belief that perfect happiness is impossible in this life; belief in the necessity of personal immortality to complete the happiness intended, apparently by nature; belief in personal immortality; belief in the special creation of individual souls; and belief in a divinely implanted "natural" habit of the moral virtues. These beliefs are not specifically Christian since they are shared by many non-Christians including Jews, Muslims, and other theists. Furthermore not all these beliefs are shared by Christians, since some Protestants reject belief in a divinely implanted natural habit of the moral virtues. But if we revise Jaffa's complaint from the importation of Christian principles to the importation of theistic principles, what should the response be in this case?

Recently, James C. Doig, in his book, *Aquinas's Philosophical Commentary on the Ethics: A Historical Perspective*, provided a detailed response to the specifics of Jaffa's critique, arguing that each of these beliefs, although also revealed, is given a philosophical foundation by Aquinas.[6] For example, although God's providence is a matter of revelation, it can also be established as true according to Aquinas on the basis of reason. Since I find Doig's argument persuasive, I will forego the specifics of Jaffa's view and assume that the *Commentary on the Ethics* is not a theological work in the sense of depending on religious faith, but that it is a properly philosophical work. Even if the commentary is a philosophical work in this sense, it still may be fruitful to explore the place of God within it.

### The Place of God in the Commentary on the Ethics

What does Aquinas specifically say about God in the *Sententia Libri Ethicorum*? Actually a great deal, including the following: God is the ultimate source of all being[7] and good[8] in whom the truth is first and chiefly found.[9] Not only does God *not* desire evil,[10] but also God's very substance contains no evil whatsoever.[11] God is the principal cause of our happiness.[12] Aquinas remarks that God's power does not extend to contradictions,[13] that the divine nature is

---

6    J. Doig, *Aquinas's Philosophical Commentary on the Ethics: A Historical Perspective* (London: Kluwer Academic Press, 2001), chapter four.

7    *In Decem Libros Ethicorum Aristotelis* 5.2.1139.

8    Ibid. 1.18.223; 1.2.30; 1.18.223.

9    Ibid. 1.6. 77.

10    Ibid. 10.12.2122.

11    Ibid. 1.6.81; 1.9.115.

12    Ibid. 1.14.169.

13    Ibid. 6.2.1139.

simple and unchangeable,[14] and that the existence and the essence of God are identical.[15] Possessing goodness perfectly in himself,[16] the Divine Being provides providential care for human affairs,[17] acts through the contemplation of truth, and confers the greatest blessings on those who love and honor their intellect.[18] Indeed, the *Commentary on the Ethics* makes more than 180 references to God, the First Mover, or the Divine.

Despite the many references, word counts do not reveal the importance, centrality, or role of the God, the First Mover, or the Divine in this commentary. Aquinas also makes frequent mention of ancient persons of fame such as Homer, Pericles, and Trajan, but the *Sentencia* as an account of ethics hardly depends on belief in, or the existence of such personages. The role the divine plays in the *Sentencia Libri Ethicorum* cannot be determined simply by counting citations, nor would this role be properly understood through a quick summary of what Aquinas says about God as stated above. Most references to the divine in the *Commentary* are digressions, said almost in passing to exclude some possible error or to expand upon a fairly tangential point. For instance the Aristotelian text in many places speaks of the "gods," and in commenting on such passages, Aquinas often reminds readers that Aristotle is referring to separated substances.[19] Although most references to the divine play only a tangential role, some references to God play important functions in a given argument, and it is these passages that I would like to examine at greater length.

The discussion will have two main parts: First, I will examine a passage that indicates knowledge of God as a separated good, which does not play an important role in ethics according to Aquinas' understanding of the *Ethics*. Next, I will bring forward a number of passages in which God does play a central role, but show why the wider argument presented in the *Sentencia Libri Ethicorum* does not depend on such passages. I hope that an examination of both of these passages will demonstrate clearly the role the divine plays in Aquinas' commentary. And thus I come to my thesis: although the moral life as presented in this work is definitely compatible with belief in God, and in fact does appeal to God in a substantive way, nevertheless theistic belief is not a necessary component or required prerequisite for the account of the moral life presented in the *Sentencia Libri Ethicorum*.

## God Cannot be the End of Moral Life

Against his friends the Platonists, Aristotle rejected this idea that ethical knowledge was derived from metaphysical knowledge. Unlike for Socrates, for

---

14   Ibid. 7.14.1535.
15   Ibid. 9.4.1807.
16   Ibid. 9.4.1807.
17   Ibid. 10.13.2133.
18   Ibid. 10.14.2138.
19   Ibid. 1.18.218.

Aristotle one does not need to know about the separated "Form" of the Good in order to have ethical knowledge of the morally good. Aquinas' argument for this conclusion begins with a reminder of what the scope of moral philosophy is. As Aquinas remarks in the commentary on the first book of the *Ethics*, in moral philosophy, we seek the end that is happiness *as able to be secured through human actions*. He writes:

> We are looking for the happiness that is the end of human acts. The end, however, of man is either some thing he does or some external thing. This can be the end of man either because it is produced, as a house is the end of building or it is possessed as a thing that is used.[20]

The end of human acts could be then one of three things. First, the end could be something an agent does, such as singing, thinking, or moving. Secondly, the end could be something an agent makes, such as a house, a boat, or a diagram. Thirdly, the end could be something an agent possesses or uses, such as looking at the beauty of the Swiss Alps, the "Romantic Rhine," or an emerald forest. Such objects of natural beauty are not themselves human actions nor are they human artifacts but a human being may *enjoy* them, and in that sense *use* or *possess* them and so derive happiness.

But human happiness as achievable by human action (*finis quo*) does not involve God as a part of any of these three ends. God is a separated good. He is not a human action like human thinking or human desiring. God is not a human creation or fabrication, as idol worshippers or sociologists of religion might suppose. Finally, God according to Thomas in the *Commentary* is not an object that could be possessed or enjoyed by human beings in this life. "Moreover, it (this separated good) does not seem to be something possessed by man as he possesses things used in this life. Obviously, then, the common or separated good is not the good of man that is the object of our present search."[21] God cannot be possessed in this life but only enjoyed in the life to come. So the separated good, God or any other, cannot be the end that is sought in the moral life as accounted for in moral philosophy.

### The Unnecessary References to God

Now I would like to examine passages where belief in God plays a substantive role in the argument. The first place the divine plays a pivotal role in Aquinas' argument is in his discussion of whether there is a final end for human beings. There must be a final end, since we cannot proceed to infinity in *desired* ends because then our desires would never be able to reach fulfillment. Natural desires cannot be in vain, so there must be some final end for human beings. Now someone might suppose that natural desires could be in vain. To this Aquinas responds: "But this is impossible. The reason is that a natural desire is

---

20   Ibid. 1.2.21.
21   Ibid. 1.8.98.

nothing else but an inclination belonging to things by disposition of the First
Mover, and thus cannot be frustrated. Therefore it is impossible that we should
proceed to an infinity of ends."[22] Natural desire cannot be in vain for it belongs
to a creature by virtue of the First Mover. About the final end of human beings,
Aquinas makes a similar argument elsewhere: "It may happen that a man is a
weaver, tanner, grammarian, musician, or anything else of the kind. In none of
these capacities does he lack a proper operation, for otherwise he would possess
them as empty and useless things. Now it is far more unfitting that a thing
ordained by divine reason, as is the naturally existent, should be unprofitable
and useless than a thing arranged by human reason. Since, therefore, man is a
being that possesses a *natural* existence, it is impossible that he should be by
nature without a purpose, or a proper operation."[23] Here we find the divine
invoked in order to support the idea that the human person has a proper operation. Without a proper operation and a natural end, a human person's desires
would be in vain including the desire for happiness, which is the basis for a
*eudemonistic* ethics. Thus the *Ethics* of Aristotle, at least as interpreted by
Aquinas, depends upon a belief in God.

But it should be noted that although Thomas does appeals to the divine at
this point, he also calls upon another argument to reach the same conclusion,
and this argument makes no reference whatsoever to God. Aquinas writes that
Aristotle:

> proves the same truth by means of human members. We must consider that
> the same mode of operation is found in the whole and in the parts of man,
> because, as the soul is the act of the whole body, so certain powers of the
> soul are acts of certain parts of the body, as sight is of the eye. But each part
> of man has a proper operation; for example, the operation of the eye is see-
> ing; and of the hand, touching; and of the feet, walking; and so of the other
> parts. We conclude, therefore, that some operation proper to man as a whole
> exists.[24]

If the individual parts of a human being have various functions by virtue of
the power of the soul, the soul's power being manifest in both the parts of the
body and the whole, then the human being as a whole must have a proper operation too. The conclusion therefore that human beings have a proper operation
does not depend on belief in God's existence since it can also be derived in a
way that does not rely on a belief in God's existence.

Secondly, the divine enters the *Sententia Libri Ethicorum* in a significant
way in Aquinas' comparison of the intellectual and practical virtues.[25] In

---

22    Ibid. I.2.21.
23    Ibid. I.10.121.
24    Ibid. I.10.122.
25    Ibid. 10.12.2121–2123.

arguing for the superiority of the intellectual virtues (and hence the life of contemplation) over the moral virtues (and hence the political life), Aquinas appeals to God's nature, as well as the nature of separated substances, as freed from all passions. Almost Anselmian in inspiration, in order to know which life and which virtues are greater than others, he appeals to that than which nothing greater can be conceived. The superiority of a given virtue is seen by its greater resemblance to God. Since God undergoes no passions, God has no need of the moral virtues. However, God does enjoy the intellectual virtues such as wisdom. So the intellectual virtues must be better than the moral virtues since the being that than which nothing greater can be conceived has one kind of virtue but not the other. So, in order to know about the superiority of the intellectual virtues over the moral, one must have knowledge of the divine.

Once again, although God plays a central role in this argument from the *Commentary*, Aquinas provides other non-theistic arguments for the same conclusion. Having established earlier that happiness is activity in accordance with the highest virtue,[26] Aquinas understands Aristotle to give a series of arguments that the activity according to the highest virtue is contemplation. None of these depend upon a belief in God, and Aquinas spends *lectio* ten of book ten treating these arguments. First, the highest operation of the intellect is the best occupation in us. We differ from the beasts not in using reason for practical affairs such as seeking food but in using reason for theoretical aims such as knowing the truth about that which lies beyond the senses. Exercise of the intellect is also the most continuous occupation we possess since bodily activity, particularly strenuous bodily activity, rather quickly makes a human being tire. Third, intellectual pleasure, unlike bodily pleasure, does not depend on a previous privation or lack and so is a more "pure" pleasure than pleasures which depend upon prior deprivations. Fourth, although contemplation is best pursued with friends, intellectual activity is highly self-sufficient unlike for instance the exercise of justice which *requires* another person. Fifth, although practical virtues may also be the means to another end (as temperance helps one finish one's work or justice helps establish peace among neighbors), contemplation is loved for its own sake, not as a means to further ends. Thus, it more especially shares in the nature of happiness as a final end. Finally, unlike the business of a person exercising practical virtue, contemplation pertains to leisureliness, a freedom from labor which is assigned to a happy person. Since none of these arguments depends upon belief in God, Thomas can establish the superiority of the exercise of contemplation over moral virtues without relying on the divine even though he does invoke the divine in order to show the superiority of intellectual over practical virtues.

A third way that God would seem to be presupposed for ethics concerns the pedagogy of philosophy. Interestingly, this pedagogy would appear at first

---

26    Ibid. 10.9.2078.

glance to support the idea that God is not required for ethics; but this argument is more complicated than the first glance would indicate. Aquinas, following Aristotle, holds that there is a proper order whereby students master certain subjects first before advancing to more difficult subjects. There is an order to learning in which the necessary prerequisites for understanding more difficult subjects are first mastered in subjects more easily understood.

> Therefore, the proper order of learning is that boys first be instructed in things pertaining to logic because logic teaches the method of the whole of philosophy. Next, they should be instructed in mathematics, which does not need experience and does not exceed the imagination. Third in natural sciences, which, even though they not exceeding sense and imagination, nevertheless require experience. Fourth, in the moral sciences, which require experience and a soul free from passions, as was noted in the first book. Fifth, in the sapiential and divine sciences, which exceed imagination and require a sharp mind.[27]

Those subjects that require very little experience are the first that should be learned such as logic and mathematics. Subjects requiring the most experience to master should only be undertaken later, such as the natural sciences. Before the *sapiential* and divine sciences, moral philosophy should be studied. And the last subject that should be studied is metaphysics. Ethics comes therefore in the middle, after logic and mathematics but before metaphysics, and therefore before a metaphysical knowledge of God. So, knowledge of God, at least as acquired in metaphysics should be acquired only after the study of ethics. This Aristotelian-Thomistic pedagogy leads to the conclusion that knowledge of God is not logically prior to ethical knowledge.

Unfortunately, a big problem arises for this line of argument. In the *Physics* commentary, an exploration pertaining to natural science, Aquinas establishes the existence of the unmoved mover, so the existence of God would be something learned *before* ethics. So even though the divine and *sapiential* sciences are explored in greatest depth in metaphysics, undertaken after moral philosophy, God's existence is established in the discipline of natural sciences, which should be undertaken before moral philosophy. So, the student who follows Aristotle's recommended pedagogy would have knowledge of God before studying the subject of moral philosophy. God is necessary for moral philosophy.

This objection however is not fatal to the position defended here. It doesn't follow from the fact that something is learned before in a particular science that what is learned is necessary for the following sciences. We also learn in natural philosophy about the characteristics of animals, but these facts are not necessary for moral philosophy. We learn the truths of geometry, but it does not follow that the truths of moral philosophy depend upon the truths of geometry. The

27    Ibid. 6.7.1121.

Aristotelian ordering of learning proves neither that God is needed for moral philosophy (nor does it show that God is *not* needed).

The final way the divine enters the *Commentary* in a central role is in the consideration of the cause of human happiness. Aquinas comments that "it is tolerable to say that happiness (*felicitas*) is from a human cause, even if principally from a divine cause, nevertheless in this man must in some way cooperate."[28] In book one, *lectio* fourteen, Aquinas considers the cause of human happiness but right away rejects fortune as the cause. Rather, happiness is caused proximately by human action but principally and first by a divine cause.[29] So, God would seem to be an essential part of *eudemonistic* ethics as its first and primary cause.

Even though the first and principle cause of human happiness is God, the proximate cause of happiness is human. That God would be the first cause of human happiness is rather obvious, since God is the first cause of all things, including the objects of geometry. But this indicates why knowledge of God is not necessarily essential to moral philosophy as understood by Aquinas. If God causes all being, then we couldn't exist without God, and if we did not exist we could not perform human actions, the concern of moral philosophy. But moral philosophy need not give an account of all the conditions necessary for the existence of human action, since then moral philosophy would also have to give an account of how our brain stem operates since we cannot perform human actions without a functioning brain stem. But surely brain stems are not a facet of moral philosophy despite being a necessary condition for any earthly human action. So too, knowledge of God as first cause is not essential to moral philosophy *simply on account* of God's existence being necessary for human action. Just as one can understand geometry without knowledge of God so too one can understand Aristotelian moral philosophy without a knowledge of God, even though in terms of the order of being, neither geometry nor human actions (the subject of moral philosophy) are possible without God. In the order of knowing, neither geometry nor ethics depend upon God; although in the order of being, both geometry and ethics depend upon God. Obviously to have a comprehensive knowledge of all things one would have to know the cause of all things, but such knowledge goes well beyond that which is required for ethics. So, the fact that

---

28  "[O]stendit tolerabiliter dici quod felicitas sit ex causa humana, quia, etiam si sit a deo principaliter, tamen adhuc homo aliquid cooperatur." *In Decem Libros Ethicorum Aristotelis* 1.14.169. Thomas uses *felicitas* to denote imperfect happiness in the Commentary and reserves *beatitudo* for what he calls 'perfect happiness' in the *Summa Theologiae*. *Beatitudo* is but rarely mentioned in *In Decem Libros Ethicorum Aristotelis* which focuses on *felicitas*.

29  "felicitas igitur non est a fortuna, sed ab aliqua causa humana proxima, a causa autem divina principaliter et primo." *In Decem Libros Ethicorum Aristotelis* 1.14.179.

Aquinas acknowledges that happiness is caused principally and first by a divine cause does not imply that this divine cause must be known or invoked in moral philosophy which seeks to understand the proximate human cause of happiness.

Another way to approach the question about God and happiness in the *Sententia Libri Ethicorum* is to note that Aquinas seeks to understand happiness in terms of the *finis quo,* the proximate cause by which a person achieves happiness and not primarily in terms of the *finis cuius,* that in which the person finds happiness. The *finis quo* of the miser is possessing money; the *finis cuius* of the miser is the money itself.[30] The *finis quo* of the intemperate person is to enjoy bodily pleasure beyond what is reasonable; the *finis cuius* is the wine, sex, or food from which the agent derives bodily pleasure. In the *Sententia Libri Ethicorum,* Aquinas is primarily exploring those actions by which a human person can achieve happiness, the *finis quo,* and this *finis quo* does not consist, as noted earlier, in the enjoyment of a separated good such as God. "Moreover, it (this separated good) does not seem to be something possessed by man as he possesses things used in this life. Obviously, then, the common or separated good is not the good of man that is the object of our present search."[31] As he makes clear in the preface, as well as within in the text itself, happiness as the proper operation of a human person (*actio humana, finis quo*) is the subject of the *Commentary on the Nicomachean Ethics.*[32]

But this response merely raises another difficulty: Even if happiness understood as a *finis quo,* that is as an operation of a human person, is a created and not an uncreated entity; nevertheless, happiness as a *finis cuius* might consist in an uncreated being, God. Even if happiness considered as a human operation consists in contemplation, which is itself a human action, this contemplation must be contemplation *of* the highest thing, namely God. Thus if happiness consists in the contemplation of the highest object by the highest human power, then human happiness at least in terms of the *finis cuius* cannot be understood without God. So, God does enter into his account of the *Ethics* in a very significant way, specifically as the final end (*finis cuius*) of all rightly ordered human action. But does Aquinas actually say this in the *Commentary?*

---

30   *ST*, I-II, q. 1, a. 8.

31   *In Decem Libros Ethicorum Aristotelis* 1.8.98.

32   "si autem aliqua res exterior dicatur esse finis, hoc non erit nisi mediante operatione, per quam scilicet homo ad rem illam attingit vel faciendo, sicut aedificator domum, aut utitur seu fruitur ea. Et sic relinquitur quod finale bonum cuiuslibet rei in eius operatione sit requirendum. Si igitur hominis est aliqua operatio propria, necesse est, quod in eius operatione propria consistat finale bonum ipsius, quod est felicitas, et ita genus felicitatis est propria operatio hominis. Si autem dicatur in aliquo alio felicitas consistere, aut hoc erit aliquid quo homo redditur idoneus ad huiusmodi operationem, aut erit aliquid ad quod per suam operationem attingit, sicut deus dicitur esse beatitudo hominis." *In Decem Libros Ethicorum Aristotelis* 1.10.119–120.

One passage in the *Sentencia* affirms the role of the divine in contemplation. In it, Aquinas clarifies more explicitly the nature of the *finis cuius,* the highest object of contemplation:

> the highest of human activities is contemplation of truth; and this is evident from the two reasons by which we judge the excellence of activity. First, on the part of the faculty that is the principle of the activity. Thus this activity is obviously the highest, as the intellect is the best element in us. Second, on the part of the object determining the species of the activity. Here too this activity is highest because, among the objects that can be known, the supersensible – especially divine objects – are the highest. And so it is in the contemplation of these objects that the perfect happiness of man consists.[33]

The *finis cuius* of human happiness is the *intelligibilia, et praecipue divina.* It is important to note the *plurality* of the objects of perfect happiness in the *Commentary*. Indeed, this passage, at least for the monotheist, would seem to prove too much in terms of the role of the divine, for the object of contemplation is not the one true God, but rather intelligible objects, and especially divine things. Therefore, God does not enter into the *finis quo* of human happiness, nor is God the sole object of happiness in terms of the *finis cuius.*

In conclusion, let us return to our question: can we be good without God? If we are to have perfect happiness and still the restlessness inside of our hearts, the answer is no. If we are to have an account of perfect happiness as undertaken by moral theology, the answer is again no. But does one always need to know about God's existence in order to come to right practical judgment (*synesis*) about what is evil to do and what is good to do? It seems that since our judgment about these things could be derived from non-theistic sources, including *synderis* or instruction by others, acknowledging God's existence does not appear to be necessary.

If we are seeking to understand theoretically how to pursue happiness in this life, as it is possible to achieve through virtuous human actions, and if the account of ethics depicted in the *Sentencia Libri Ethicorum* is correct, then again we can be good without believing in God. Although the Divine Being is frequently mentioned by Aquinas in the *Sentencia Libri Ethicorum,* the

---

33  "Optima autem inter operationes humanas est speculatio veritatis. Et hoc patet ex duobus, ex quibus pensatur dignitas operationis. uno modo ex parte potentiae, quae est operationis principium. Et sic patet hanc operationem esse optimam, sicut et intellectus est optimum eorum quae in nobis sunt, ut prius ostensum est. Alio modo ex parte obiecti, quod dat speciem operationi. Et secundum hoc etiam haec operatio est optima; quia inter omnia cognoscibilia optima sunt intelligibilia, et praecipue divina. Et sic in eorum speculatione consistit perfecta humana felicitas." *In Decem Libros Ethicorum Aristotelis* 10.10.2087; altered translation.

commentary makes clear that knowledge of this separated Good is not necessary for ethics. In several places where God does play a central role in the *Commentary*, Aquinas establishes the same conclusions via non-theistic arguments as well. Thus, both an atheist and a theist could in principle agree that the *Nicomachean Ethics*, as understood by Thomas Aquinas, provides a rational account of the ethical life.

# Contemplation As The End of Human Nature in Aquinas's *Sententia libri Ethicorum*

## Antonio Donato

### Introduction

One of the major philosophical challenges for Aquinas and his contemporaries was to assimilate the established ethical views of Patristic thought with both Aristotelian ethics, which had recently appeared on the scene, and the Neoplatonic views of Pseudo-Dionysius and of the *Liber De Causis*, which were also becoming rather important at the time.

Thus, an analysis of the sources of Aquinas's theory of contemplation has to take into account the diverse kinds of doctrines Aquinas was familiar with. The point of this paper is to argue that Aquinas's theory of contemplation is the result of an original dialogue among different philosophical traditions. To this end, I shall concentrate mainly on the *Sententia libri Ethicorum,* since this text seems to illustrate rather clearly how Aquinas tries to harmonize his different sources.

In this study I will proceed as follows. The first part will explain how and to what extent Aquinas's and Aristotle's doctrines of contemplation are different, despite their apparent similarity. The second part will discuss the opinions of contemporary interpreters concerning the reasons Aquinas differs from Aristotle. The third part will focus on some texts of the *Sententia libri Ethicorum* to assess which steps Aquinas takes to turn Aristotle's theory of contemplation into his own view. Finally, I shall argue that Aquinas changes Aristotle's view because of Aquinas's familiarity with some Neoplatonic doctrines, and I will focus in particular on some texts of Augustine, Pseudo-Dionysius, and the *Liber De Causis*.

### I. How Aristotle's *Theoria* Differs from Aquinas's Contemplation

Among the philosophers of the 13th century, Aquinas was one of the first to emphasize the importance of a key doctrine of the *Nicomachean Ethics* mostly underestimated by other philosophers, i.e. contemplative activity. However, although Aquinas was correct in showing the intellectualist character of Aristotelian ethics, he seems to have read Aristotle's notion of contemplation in a way not totally faithful to Aristotle. A careful comparison between a relevant passage of chapter seven of book ten of the *Nicomachean Ethics* and a text of Aquinas's *corpus* suggests that, despite the similarity that an initial analysis may suggest, Aquinas turns Aristotle's theory of *theoria* (contemplation) into a new one. In lines 1177a 10–20 Aristotle describes contemplation as follows:

> If happiness is an activity in accordance with virtue, it is reasonable that it should be in accordance with the highest virtue; and this will be the virtue of the best part in us. Whether this part be the intellect or something else that seems to rule and control us by nature and to understand noble and divine things, whether it be itself divine or the most divine element in us, the activity of this part in accordance with its proper virtue will constitute perfect happiness. Now we have already said that this activity is contemplative – a conclusion in harmony both with our previous discussion and with the truth. For contemplation is the highest operation, since the intellect is the best element in us and the objects of the intellect are the best of the things that can be known.[1]

In this text, relying on his theory according to which the end of human nature is happiness, seen as the performance of the most virtuous activity, Aristotle considers the case of *theoria*. *Theoria* may be regarded as a good candidate for being the end of human nature because of both its nature and its objects.

Firstly, Aristotle claims that *theoria* is the supreme end of human nature because of the kind of activity it involves. According with one of the most common readings, *theoria* could be regarded as the process of reflection on a system of truths already discovered.[2] Evidence of this interpretation can be found in the terminological difference between *episteme* and *theoria*. For *episteme* indicates the mere possession of correct conclusions and the ability to see how some individual items of knowledge would fit within the whole systematic context in which they are embedded. Conversely, *theoria* expresses the attitude of someone who enjoys the clear overview of the knowledge he possesses. Thus, according to this view, *theoria* is the appreciation of the knowledge already acquired.[3]

---

1    Aristotle, *Nicomachean Ethics*, X, 7, 1177a 10–20, rec. I. Bywater, OCT (Oxford, 1895).

2    Cf. W.D. Ross, *Aristotle* (London: Methuen, 1949); J. Barnes, *Ethics,* in *The Ethics of Aristotle: the Nicomachean Ethics* (Harmondsworth: Penguin, 1976).

3    According to a different interpretation Aristotle's *theoria* is the activity of searching the truths of some theoretical discipline. e. g. mathematics or philosophy. Hence, *theoria* would be an exercise of discursive reasoning, an intellectual research which logically moves from known premises to hitherto unknown conclusions. Thus, the

Secondly, Aristotle holds that *theoria* may be seen as the supreme end of human life, since it is what is divine. It seems that traditionally scholars have overemphasised this claim, suggesting that since the best object of *theoria* is the divine, *theoria* consists only in the reflection on theological or astronomical propositions and their proofs.[4] This interpretation runs the risk of restricting *theoria* to theology and astronomy only, excluding all the other theoretical sciences. On the contrary, it appears plausible that Aristotle here does not imply any precise or technical notion of God or of the divine; rather, he relies on the intuition that the object of *theoria* is what is noblest and most true. This interpretation has the advantage of providing a broader notion of *theoria* suitable to include all the theoretical sciences.

Considering now Aquinas's own doctrine, we can see that he adopted a eudaemonological and teleological standpoint as well as an intellectualist theory of the end of human nature quite close to Aristotle's view.[5] Nevertheless, a crucial text of Aquinas's *corpus* suggests a difference between Aquinas's and Aristotle's theories.

By the name of beatitude is understood the ultimate perfection of rational or of intellectual nature; and hence it is that it is naturally desired, since everything naturally desires its ultimate perfection. Now there is a twofold ultimate perfection of rational or of intellectual nature. The first is one which it can procure of its own natural power; and this is in a measure called beatitude or happiness. Hence Aristotle (*Ethic.* x) says that man's ultimate happiness consists in his most perfect contemplation, whereby in this life he can behold the best intelligible object; and that is God. Above this happiness there is still another, which we look forward to in the future, whereby "we shall see God as He is." This is beyond the nature of every created intellect, as was shown above.[6]

---

pleasure of this activity would consists in conducting research hoping in some discoveries in the broad field of knowledge and in rejoicing in each advance that it is made. Cf. W.F.R. Hardie, *Aristotle's Ethical Theory*, 2nd ed. (Oxford, Clarendon Press, 1980); W.K.C. Guthrie, *A History of Greek Philosophy* (Cambridge: Cambridge University Press, 1981), vol. VI.

4   Cf. S. Broadie, *Ethics with Aristotle* (Oxford: Oxford University Press, 1991).
5   For a detailed account of Aquinas's theory of contemplation see: A. Donagan, *Human Ends and Human Actions: an Exploration in St. Thomas's Treatment* (Milwaukee: Marquette University Press, 1985); R. Pasnau and C. Shields, *The Philosophy of Aquinas* (Boulder: Westview Press, 2004), 197–217.
6   *Summa Theologiae,* I, q. 62, a 1, in *Opera Omnia*, Leonina, Roma, 1888–1906, tt. 4–12: "Respondeo dicendum quod nomine beatitudinis intelligitur ultima perfectio rationalis seu intellectualis naturae, et inde est quod naturaliter desideratur, quia unumquodque naturaliter desiderat suam ultimam perfectionem. Ultima autem perfectio rationalis seu intellectualis naturae est duplex. Una quidem, quam potest

This text illustrates how Aquinas turns Aristotle's doctrine into a different one. Aquinas introduces a distinction between two ways in which contemplation may occur: an imperfect one, attainable in this life, which is accomplished by the considerations of the speculative sciences, and a perfect one, possible only in the afterlife, consisting in the vision of God. Aquinas attributes to Aristotle the notion of imperfect contemplation, which is neither mentioned nor implied by Aristotle. Hence, Aquinas regards Aristotle's contemplation as imperfect and presents a new way in which contemplation may occur, unknown to Aristotle, that he considers the perfect one and, consequently, the end of human nature. In Aquinas's perspective the distinction between the two ways of contemplation is necessary for several reasons. First, because Aquinas's view of perfect contemplation consists in the uninterrupted vision of God, which is not possible in this life. Second, for Aquinas, in this life man can only attain an imperfect and analogical notion of God's nature.

Furthermore, it should be noticed that for Aquinas contemplation seems to diverge from Aristotle's *theoria* in three crucial respects: as kinds of activity, in relation to human nature, and with respect to their content.

Firstly, for Aquinas contemplation is regarded as a different kind of activity from Aristotle's *theoria,* since it is not the philosophical reflection on supreme truths, but rather a vision which outstrips the resources of metaphysical knowledge. It is, indeed, the immediate cognitive awareness of God, who transcends the entire order of the universe.

Secondly, Aquinas's notion of contemplation and Aristotle's *theoria* are different also concerning their nature. Aquinas maintains that the end of human nature is the fulfillment of man's natural desire, i.e., the vision of God, that can be attained only in the next world. On the contrary, *theoria* consists in performing the most virtuous and enjoyable activity. In Aristotle, indeed, *theoria* is the source of happiness because it is the kind of activity that it is most proper to human beings. Aristotle does not think that man's purpose is the vision of God in the next world.

Thirdly, Aquinas's contemplation differs from Aristotle's *theoria* also concerning its content. In Aristotle the content of *theoria* is the divine in a very extended sense: namely, the contemplation of supreme truths. Conversely, in Aquinas the content of contemplation seems to have a much more precise target, namely the vision of God.

By comparing some of Aristotle's and Aquinas's crucial texts we can deter-

---

assequi virtute suae naturae, et haec quodammodo beatitudo vel felicitas dicitur. Unde et Aristoteles perfectissimam hominis contemplationem, qua optimum intelligibile, quod est Deus, contemplari potest in hac vita, dicit esse ultimam hominis felicitatem. Sed super hanc felicitatem est alia felicitas, quam in futuro expectamus, qua videbimus Deum sicuti est. Quod quidem est supra cuiuslibet intellectus creati naturam, ut supra ostensum est". See also: *In Quattuor Libros Sententiarum,* q. 1 a. 1 co, P. Madonnet ed., 2t., Parigi 1929.

mine the difference between their notions of contemplation. However, the simple comparison of the two theories is not enough to see why this difference emerges. The analysis of most of the opinions of major scholars on the topic and the careful consideration of their arguments are relevant to a better understanding of the complexity and articulation of the problem.

## II. *Status Quaestionis* on the Way in which Aristotle's *Theoria* Turned into Aquinas's *Contemplation*

The attempt to explain Aquinas's change of Aristotle's theory has led scholars to two rather different interpretations, which could be labeled as *philosophical* and *theological*.

According to the philosophical one – put forward by Elders, Kleber and Doig – Aquinas changes Aristotle on a purely philosophical basis, following the *intentio auctoris*, namely, trying to make explicit Aristotle's intent.[7] This interpretation is well supported by a recent work of Doig who proposes that Aquinas, while trying to explicate the *intentio auctoris*, completed the Aristotelian doctrine of contemplation as the ultimate end of human nature in a way Aristotle never intended.[8] To illustrate his view Doig argues that when Aristotle in the *Nicomachean Ethics* I. 10 considers whether someone can be considered happy while still alive he advances a doctrine very similar to Aquinas's. Hence, when Aristotle observes that some men are called "blessed" he adds the qualification that he is speaking about being blessed only "as men."[9] In Doig's reading, this implies that Aristotle himself recognise that this worldly happiness, based on contemplation, is imperfect. Given that way of interpreting Aristotle, Doig can then easily show that Aquinas's theory of the two kinds of contemplation is only a rather natural development of Aristotle. Therefore, he can conclude that:

> By tracing Aquinas use of the expression (blessed as men) we discovered that he completed Aristotle's doctrine of human happiness, not by interjection of some Christian belief, but by addition of his own philosophically argued conviction that perfect happiness is open to man after death.[10]

---

7    Cf. L. Elders, *Saint Thomas Aquinas's Commentary on The Nicomachean Ethics,* in *Autour de saint Thomas d'Aquin: recueil d'études sur sa pensée philosophique et théologique* (FAC Tabor, Paris Brugge, 1987), 77–142; *Saint Thomas d'Aquin et Aristote,* "Revue thomiste," 96 (1988): 357–76; H. Kleber, *Glück als Lebenziel: Untersuchungen zur Philosophie des Glücks bei Thomas von Aquin,* Aschendorff (Münster, 1988); J.C. Doig, *Aquinas's philosophical commentary on the Ethics: a historical perspective* (Dordrecht/London: Kluwer Academic Publishers, 2001).

8    Doig 2001.

9    Cf. Aquinas's *Commentary,* ¶202, and *Summa Theologiae* I-II, q. 5, a. 4, and q. 3, a. 2, ad 4.

10   Doig 2001, 135

Similarly, Kleber holds that Aquinas attributes to Aristotle some new philosophical principles.[11] This seems to be part of Aquinas's approach to endeavouring to discover the *intentio auctoris*, while always keeping in mind the *veritas rei*. In order to support this view Kleber distinguishes between insights of theology and insights due to the knowledge of revelation and implies that the latter are responsible of the development of Aquinas's theory of two kinds of happiness.

By contrast, the theological reading – supported by Copleston, Jaffa, Gauthier, Owens, Wieland, Jordan, Thiry, Torrell, and Bradley – claims that Aquinas's modification is due to his theological attitude of interpreting Aristotle in the light of Christian beliefs.[12] The views of the interpreters who sustain the theological interpretation are not as homogeneous as those of the scholars in favor of the philosophical one. For that matter, two quite different views can be distinguished: an extreme and a moderate one. The moderate view (Copleston, Jaffa, Wieland and Thiry) proposes that Aquinas's change of Aristotle is due to his "apostolic perspective" in reading Aristotle. On the other hand, the extreme view (Gauthier, Owens, Jordan, Torrell and Bradley) maintains that Aquinas's change is due to theological reasons only, totally extraneous to Aristotle.

---

11    Kleber 1988.
12    Cf. Copleston F., *History of Philosophy* (London: Burns & Oates Search Press, 1950), vol. II; H.V. Jaffa, *Thomism and aristotelism. A study of the Commentary by Thomas Aquinas on the Nicomachean Ethics* (Chicago: University of Chicago Press, 1952); R.A. Gauthier and J.Y. Jolif, *L'Éthique à Nicomaque. Introduction, Traduction et Commentaire* (Louvain: Publications universitaires, 1958–1959); J. Owens, "Aquinas as Aristotelian Commentator," in *St. Thomas Aquinas, 1274–1974: Commemorative Studies* (Toronto: Pontifical Institute of Mediaeval Studies, 1974), 213–38; G. Wieland, *Ethica, scientia practica: die Anfänge der philosophischen Ethik im 13. Jahrhundert* (Aschendorff, Münster Westfalen, 1981); "Happiness: the perfection of man," in *The Cambridge History of Later Medieval Philosophy*, ed. N. Kretzmann, E. Stump, and J. Pinborg (Cambridge: Cambridge University Press, 1982), 673–87; "The reception and interpretation of Aristotle's Ethics," in Kretzmann et al., 657–73; A. Thiry, "Saint Thomas et la morale d'Aristote," in *Autour de saint Thomas d'Aquin: recueil d'études sur sa pensée philosophique et théologique* (FAC Tabor, Paris Brugge), 1987; M. Jordan, "Aquinas Reading Aristotle's Ethics," in *Ad litteram: authoritative texts and their medieval readers* (Notre Dame, IN: University of Notre Dame Press, 1992), 229–49; "Theology and Philosophy" in *The Cambridge Companion to Aquinas,* ed.N. Kretzmann and E. Stump (Cambridge: Cambridge University Press, 1993), 232–51; J.P. Torrell, *Initiation à Saint Thomas d'Aquin. Sa personne et son oeuvre* (Paris: Editiones De Cerf, 1993); D.J.M. Bradley, *Aquinas on the twofold human good: reason and human happiness in Aquinas's moral science* (Washington: Catholic University of America Press, 1997).

One of the most exhaustive accounts of the extreme view may be found in Bradley.[13] He underlines that if human nature is studied in the light of its orientation toward its ultimate end, i.e. the vision of God in another life, then Aquinas's ethics is fundamentally theological. Thus, Aquinas's theory is the result of his theological beliefs and, as a Christian philosopher, Aquinas has to offer a doctrine of the end of human nature based on a perspective aided by faith.[14]

Among the proponents of the extreme view, Owens' reading was one of the first and most influential.[15] He remarks that Aristotelian ethics, in describing happiness as an intellectual activity, offers a good means to express the theological doctrine of contemplation. However, the requirements that Aristotle adds to the exercise of *theoria* – friends, affluence, good looks, honor, etc. – could not apply to the Christian ultimate end. Hence, Aquinas has to regard Aristotelian contemplation as an imperfect one which needs to be completed by a higher one, the perfect contemplation, which is the proper end of human nature. Therefore, Aquinas has to put within an Aristotelian framework the beliefs of the Christian tradition to which he belongs. Owens stresses the theological direction of Aquinas's reading of Aristotle, noticing:

> These considerations (theological) dominate Thomistic interpretation of Aristotle [...] They seem to generate theology, not philosophy. The purpose is to defend revealed truth, not just Christian philosophical truth.[16]

One of the best representatives of the moderate view is Jaffa, who advances the argument that Aquinas, although maintaining Aristotle's doctrine, proposes a development of Aristotle's doctrine that is Christian and theological.[17] Jaffa, moreover, considers the problem of how Aquinas can introduce the doctrine of the kinds of contemplation, taking into account the same Aristotelian text studied by Doig. Differently from Doig, he does not think that the formula "blessed as men" can be interpreted in Aquinas's sense. This would be to ignore the context in which this discussion is contained. In these lines of Book I, indeed, Aristotle is discussing the characteristics of the moral life and its peculiarity, whilst the contemplative life will be considered only later. Hence, Aquinas's use of the formula "blessed as men" to make room for the doctrine of the two kinds of contemplation adds something to the text. Thus, in Jaffa's view, this is a clear case in which Aquinas has to change Aristotle's perspective because of his Christian principle. He says:

---

13  Bradley 1997.
14  Bradley 1997, 30–31
15  Owens 1974.
16  Owens 1974, 238
17  Jaffa 1952.

> We conclude then that Thomas' assumption as to harmony of natural and
> revealed doctrine, at least in so far as Aristotle is to be considered a
> representative of the former, is entirely unwarranted. Thomas' "success" in
> creating the appearance of such harmony, is due, we believed, entirely to his
> imputation to Aristotle of such non-Aristotelian principles.[18]

In a like manner, Copleston takes the view that, although Aquinas's conception has in common with Aristotle both the intellectualist and the theological
approach, he considerably varies Aristotle's notion of the end of human nature.[19]
In order to do that, Copleston emphasizes, Aquinas acted as both theologian and
philosopher, presupposing some theological doctrines and trying to make them
fit in his Aristotelian philosophical framework.

Each of these interpretations of how Aquinas turns Aristotle's *theoria* into
*beatitudo* involves some difficulties. The philosophical interpretation holds that
Aquinas introduces ideas extraneous to Aristotle but as a result of philosophical
reasons only. However, this is not too easy to see since these scholars admit that
the ideas mentioned (perfect happiness, *beatitudo*, vision of God) and the
change inserted (the two ways of contemplation) are understandable within a
theological framework only. In much the same way, the theological reading, in
both its extreme and moderate versions, is not totally free of difficulties. First,
it is not too convincing to claim, as the extreme view does, that Aquinas modifies Aristotle on a purely theological basis by introducing in ethics theological
principles totally extraneous to the realm of ethics. Secondly, the exponents of
moderate view should have explained more fully what exactly Aquinas's "apostolic perspective" in reading Aristotle is.[20]

The difficulties involved in these various interpretations offer evidence for
the importance of trying to consider other factors that could have played a role
in Aquinas's modification of the Aristotelian view. More generally, following
the different interpretations, it is not evident how Aquinas could possibly introduce his Christian principles without substantially modifying Aristotle's theory.[21] These difficulties suggest the importance of considering other factors that
could have played a role in Aquinas's appropriation of Aristotelian *theoria*.

### III. Aquinas's Theory of Contemplation in the *Sententia libri Ethicorum*

Perhaps we should consider that Aquinas's theory is grounded in a philosophical view alternative to Aristotle's, one which, I think, emerges clearly in the
*Sententia libri Ethicorum* (henceforth SLE).

---

18   Jaffa 1952, 187.
19   Copleston 1950.
20   Cf. Copleston 1950.
21   See in particoular Jaffa 1952.

Several things suggest the relevance of the SLE to our inquiry. The first is its composition. According to Gauthier, the SLE was composed in 1272–73; thus it is a rather mature work and it was written after *Summa Theologiae Primae Secundae*.[22] As a later work, it offers quite good evidence of Aquinas's interpretation of Aristotle. The second relevance of the SLE is its form. The genre of a commentary makes the text particularly suitable to illustrate how and when Aquinas modifies Aristotle.

The impression that Aquinas's doctrine of contemplation is an alternative to Aristotle's *theoria,* and not just its evolution or updated version, is suggested by its being grounded in a rather different philosophical view. More precisely, a different understanding of the nature of ethics.

Aquinas provides a very intellectualist interpretation of Aristotle's ethics, significantly different not only from Aristotle's text but also from the most common view of Aquinas's predecessors and contemporaries. Aquinas differs from Aristotle, who allows two goals for human life, i.e. contemplation and political activity,[23] by claiming that there is only a single goal for human life, viz. contemplation. Consequently, Aquinas implies that not only the best decision in every situation is that which most conduces to contemplation, but also that the exercise of practical virtue is a path towards contemplation. By contrast, Aristotle does not believe that actions are valuable for the promotion of contemplation or that practical decisions are to be judged by their contribution to the achievement of contemplation. Aquinas also differs from the established view supported by Eustratius, Averroes and Albert. For, despite their differences, they all emphasize the role of political life, since they consider political life to be what is proper to a human agent. Consequently, they reject the contemplative life as solitary, more divine than human, and less appropriate as the end of human life.

Given the difference between Aquinas's and Aristotle's views, it is difficult to see how Aquinas's doctrine of contemplation can be fully compatible with Aristotle's *theoria.* It seems to be much more a radical change than a natural development. A study of SLE can illustrate the four steps in which Aquinas transforms Aristotle.

The first step consists in making room for his doctrine of contemplation. Starting from Aristotle's idea that contemplation is one of the ends of human nature, and consequently the happiest activity, Aquinas introduces a problem unknown to Aristotle, namely that perfect happiness and perfect contemplation do not appear to be possible in this life.

---

22   Gauthier and Jolif, 1958–1959.

23   Cf. Gauthier R. A. et Jolif, 1958–1959; J.L. Ackrill, "Aristotle on Eudaimonia" in A. O. Rorty, *Essays on Aristotle's Ethics* (Berkeley: University of California Press, 1980), 15–35; T. Nagel, "Aristotle on Eudaimonia," in Rorty 1980, 7–14; A..O. Rorty, "The Place of Contemplation in Aristotle's Nicomachean Ethics," in Rorty 1980, 395–436; J.O. Urmson, *Aristotle's Ethics* (Oxford: Blackwell, 1988); S.

In this work the Philosopher speaks of happiness as it is attainable in this life, for happiness in a future life is entirely beyond the investigation of reason.[24]

Aquinas indicates that complete happiness is not achievable in this life because the full contemplation of God, that is perfect happiness, it is not possible to human beings in this life. Aquinas's view is grounded on his theory of the impossibility of knowing the essence or the nature of God. This is due mainly to the idea that God himself is infinite knowledge, whereas every created intellect has a limited capacity to know. This view relies on the principle according to which the object of knowledge, in so far as it is to be known, has to be in due proportion to the cognitive capacity of the knower. Our knowledge is commensurate with finite realities and cannot attain the infinity of God's nature.[25] Furthermore, the essential dependence of human knowledge on bodily capabilities makes the vision of the divine essence impossible under the conditions of this life. Thus, since in this life our knowledge of God's nature is imperfect, God can be known only indirectly. Therefore, perfect contemplation and complete happiness cannot be attained in this life.

Nevertheless, since every human being desires to see God in his essence, this desire cannot be frustrated by the incapacity of human beings to reach the essence of God. Otherwise, the absurd conclusion would be drawn that human beings are created to achieve an end, contemplation, that is for them unreachable. In order to overcome this difficulty, Aquinas introduces an element extraneous to Aristotle, namely the doctrine of the two ways of happiness and contemplation. Thus, Aquinas's second step is to introduce the need for a new type of contemplation.

But because these things seem not to measure up in all respects to the conditions required for happiness above, he adds that those we call happy are men, subject to change in this life, who cannot attain perfect beatitude. Since a natural desire is not in vain, we can correctly judge that perfect beatitude is reserved for man after this life. He concludes with the remark that we have said enough on these points.[26]

24  *Sententia Libri Ethicorum* L I, l. IX, 113 (henceforth *SLE*), *Opera Omnia,* Leonina, Roma, 1969, tt. 47. "Loquitur enim in hoc libro philosophus de felicitate, qualis in hac vita potest haberi. Nam felicitas alterius vitae omnem investigationem rationis excedit."

25  See also: *De Potentia* 7, 5; *In Librum Beati Dionysii De divinis nominibus expositio,* ed. C. Pera-P. Caramello-C. Mazzantini, Taurini-Romae, 1950, I, iii, 104; VII, iv, 729; I, iii, 77; *S. Th.,* 1. 13. 1; *In Sent.,* 1, 3, 1, 3; I, d. 8, q. 1 ad 4; I, d. 22, q. 1, a. 1; *Summa contra Gentiles,* Leonina, tt. XIII-XVI, Roma, 1930, I, 9; I, 14.

26  *SLE* L I, l. 16, 202: "Sed quia ista videntur non usquequaque attingere ad conditiones supra de felicitate positas, subdit quod tales dicimus beatos sicut homines, qui in hac vita mutabilitati subiecta non possunt perfectam beatitudinem habere. Et

This text suggests how, although human beings can contemplate God, under the conditions of the present life this contemplation is neither permanent nor simple, since it is repeatedly interrupted and has always to begin anew. Complete contemplation cannot exist in the present life, but God promises it to us in a future life. To hold this doctrine Aquinas suggests that Aristotle's theory is a description of the kind of contemplation possible under human conditions. Then, Aquinas fills the gap left by Aristotle's view, which does not give a description of complete contemplation.

Aquinas's discussion of the two ways of contemplation relies on his idea that happiness consists more in a speculative rather than in a practical activity. For, if the vision of God's nature is the final end of human life, then the best activity can only consist in contemplation, viz., the activity of the speculative intellect. Hence, the activity of the practical intellect can be the end for a person only in so far as it provides the proper conditions to be, ultimately, involved in contemplation.

Aquinas's third step is to suggest that contemplation is the supreme end of human life through the emphasis on the intellectual life and the consequent underestimation of the political one. This results in a radical change of one of the key points of Aristotle's ethics, viz., *phronesis*.

> We must consider that prudence is not only in the reason but has a function likewise in the appetitive faculty. Therefore, everything mentioned here is a species of prudence, to the extent that it does not reside in the reason alone but has ramifications in the appetitive faculty.[27]

In these lines we see that, in Aquinas's reading, *phronesis* (*prudentia* in Latin) loses not only the crucial role it has for Aristotle, but also its high status among the other virtues. This is due to Aquinas's view according to which the supreme end of human life is only contemplation and that the knowledge of the end can be attained only by the highest intellectual virtue, i.e., wisdom. By contrast, in Aristotle – where both the contemplative and political life are the end of human life – *phronesis* is as important as wisdom. The knowledge of the end of political life is due to the practical intellect, *phronesis*, while wisdom cannot

---

quia non est inane naturae desiderium, recte aestimari potest quod reservatur homini perfecta beatitudo post hanc vitam. Ultimo epilogat dicens, quod de his in tantum dictum sit."

27   *SLE* L VI, l. 6, 1200: "Deinde cum dicit: videtur autem etc., agit de prudentia. Et primo ostendit quae dicatur prudentia. Secundo infert quoddam corollarium ex dictis, ibi, species quidem igitur et cetera. Dicit ergo primo, quod quamvis politica tam legis positiva quam executiva sit prudentia, tamen maxime videtur esse prudentia quae est circa unum tantum, scilicet circa seipsum. Et talis ratio suiipsius gubernativa retinet sibi commune nomen prudentiae; quia aliae partes prudentiae habent propria nomina, quibus nominantur."

reach the knowledge of this end. Thus, in Aristotle, *phronesis* guides the political life, while wisdom the contemplative. On the contrary, for Aquinas, life is ordered towards its end by wisdom only.

The intellectualist approach towards ethics Aquinas carries out needs a strong grounding in order fully to justify his theory. This grounding is given by the notion of the intellect as a sort of spiritual substance. In the SLE, through a radical and extreme interpretation of some passages, Aquinas illustrates the spiritual nature of human intellect focusing on its nature, its ontological status, and its activity. Thus, Aquinas's fourth step is to suggest why contemplation is possible for the human intellect.

Firstly, Aquinas takes full advantage of Aristotle's qualification of human intellect as "divine" to claim that the human intellect has the same nature as separate substances.

> Secondly, he offers some indications of the intellect's superiority by comparison with higher or divine things to which the intellect is compared in a twofold manner. First, by a special relation to these objects: only the intellect understands things that are essentially noble or divine. In the other way the human intellect is compared to divine things by a natural affinity for them – in a different fashion corresponding to the knowledge of different objects.[28]

The signs of the excellence of the intellect are shown by a comparison with higher beings, namely divine beings. Thanks to this correlation, it emerges that the human intellect is compared with divine things because it shares a common nature with them. However, this does not mean that human intellect is identical with divine beings, but rather that the intellect is both proportionate to the divine and its activity is directed towards it.

Later Aquinas is more precise on how the claim about the divinity of the intellect should be understood:

> Others, like Aristotle, considered the intellect a part of the soul; and in this view the intellect is not something divine by itself (*simpliciter*) but the most divine of all the things in us. This is so because of its greater agreement with the separated substances, inasmuch as its activity exists without a bodily organ.[29]

---

28  *SLE* L X, l. 10, 2083: "Secundo vero, ponit signa excellentiae intellectus per comparationem ad superiora, scilicet ad res divinas, ad quas dupliciter comparatur. Uno modo secundum habitudinem, quasi ad obiecta. Solus enim intellectus habet intelligentiam de rebus essentialiter bonis, quae sunt res divinae. Alio modo comparatur intellectus humanus ad res divinas, secundum connaturalitatem ad ipsas, diversimode quidem secundum diversorum sententias."

29  *SLE* L X, l. 10, 2084: "Alii vero intellectum partem animae posuerunt, sicut Aristoteles. Et secundum hoc intellectus non est simpliciter quiddam divinum, sed

The intellect is not simply divine; it is the most divine thing in us since, like separate substances, its operations take place without any corporeal organ. Thus, Aquinas's second move is to illustrate that the human soul may be regarded as a spiritual substance because of the characteristics of its best activity. According to Aquinas, the human soul is on the borderline between corporeal and separated substances. Like angels, it engages in contemplation but, like lower beings, it busies itself with bodily activities. The human soul has, indeed, a double character. First, unlike lower beings, due to its intellectual nature it can give itself to the contemplation of supreme truths as do purely immaterial angels. Second, like any corporeal beings, it is involved in more practical activities. However, this view does not seem to be Aristotelian. The point Aristotle makes is to emphasise the excellence of the intellect. Hence, in saying that the intellect is "divine" Aristotle is not interested in suggesting any ontological similarity between the human intellect and separate substances, as Aquinas does.

Finally, focusing on the activity of the intellect, Aquinas introduces the notion of the participation of the intellect in separate substances, which prepares and renders more plausible the theory of contemplation.

> For this reason in explaining his statement he adds that man living in this manner, i.e., occupied in contemplation, does not live as man, composed of diverse elements, but as something divine is present in him, partaking in a likeness to the divine intellect.[30]

Here Aquinas claims that our knowledge of divine realties is not by abstraction, as in the case of sensible things, but rather by participation. Our intellect participates in the intellectual power of the divine, and in contemplating God it becomes in a sense one with him; it is assimilated to him, being "informed" by him. In other words, Aquinas expresses this relation in terms of his own noetic, relying on his view that the intellect in act is in a way identical with the object of knowledge as it is actually known. The departure from Aristotle is clear, since Aristotle never refers either to a common nature or to a participation between human beings and the divine.

This analysis of some texts of the SLE has shown that Aquinas's transformation of Aristotle's *theoria* into a different doctrine is grounded in a rather different philosophical perspective. This process takes place, as we have seen, in four related steps which do not make Aquinas's changes to appear as radical as they actually are.

---

    est divinissimum inter omnia quae in nobis, propter maiorem convenientiam quam habet cum substantiis separatis, secundum quod eius operatio est sine organo corporeo."

30   *SLE* L X, l. 11, 2106 "Et ideo manifestans quod dictum est, subdit quod homo sic vivens, scilicet vacando contemplationi, non vivit secundum quod homo, qui est compositus ex diversis, sed secundum quod aliquid divinum in ipso existit, prout scilicet secundum intellectum divinam similitudinem participat."

## IV. The Neoplatonic Sources of Aquinas's Theory of Contemplation

The analysis carried out so far has demonstrated Aquinas's theory of contemplation to be neither only a development nor an adjustment of Aristotle's doctrine
of *theoria* in the light of some new philosophical or theological beliefs.
However, this does not mean that Aquinas offers a brand new theory totally
unrelated to the previous philosophical discussion. Aquinas's theory of contemplation appears rather to be the result of an original and personal dialogue with
different authors deeply influenced by the Neoplatonic perspective, e.g.,
Augustine, Pseudo-Dionysius and the *Liber de Causis*.

A full and definitive account of how Aquinas reads and interprets the
Neoplatonic doctrines which are relevant to his theory of contemplation, would
be too long and complex for the purposes of this paper. Here, my goal is only to
outline how some Neoplatonic views may have played a significant role in the
development of Aquinas's theory of contemplation. My aim is not to claim that
Aquinas's notion of contemplation is a Neoplatonic doctrine, but rather that
Aquinas's difference from Aristotle's *theoria* may be better understood through
reference to some philosophical theories of Augustine, Pseudo-Dionysius, and
the *Liber de Causis*.

The premises and the framework which inform Aquinas's theory of contemplation can be found in Augustine's doctrine that there is no complete happiness
in this world and that, consequently, true happiness is to be found only in the
enjoyment of the contemplation of God in the world to come. *Retractationes* 4,
3 and I, 14, 2 provides a very good illustration of this theory:

> Si illi qui iam inuenerunt, quos in ipsa possessione iam esse diximus, sic
> accipiantur beatissimi, ut non hac vita, sed in ea quam speramus et ad quam
> per fidei viam tendimus sint, non habet iste sensus errorem. Ipsi enim iudi-
> candi sunt quod quaerendum est invenisse, qui iam ibi sunt quo nos quaren-
> do et credendo, id est viam fidei tenendo, cupimus pervenire. Si autem in
> hac vita putantur esse isti vel fuisse, id verum esse non mihi videtur, non
> quia in hac vita nihil omnino inveniri potest, quod mente cernatur non fide
> credatur, sed quia tantum est quidquid est, ut non faciat beatissimos. [...] In
> hac enim vita, quantumcumque id sciatur, nondum est beatissimum, quoni-
> am inconparabiliter longe est amplius quod inde nescitur.[31]

This text claims that perfect virtue cannot be attained in this life but only in
the next, and that happiness in this life depends strictly on the state of one's soul,
so that a wise man is happy regardless of the condition of his body. For the only
life deservedly called happy is the one in which the body cannot suffer or die
and obeys the mind without resistance. Hence, even a life devoted to philosophy
cannot give the complete knowledge of God and true happiness; complete hap-

---

31   Augustine, *Retractationes* I, 14, 2.

piness, which consists in the perfect knowledge of God, is attainable only in the future life.

The claim of the impossibility of complete happiness in this life, and thus of perfect contemplation, is sustained, according to Aquinas, by a further philosophical point. Aquinas finds in the Neoplatonic doctrine of the unknowability of God's nature, supported by both Pseudo-Dionysius and the *Liber de Causis*, the argument he needs.

In the *Commentary on Pseudo-Dionysius' De Divinis Nominibus*, Aquinas depicts with approval Pseudo-Dionysius' theory according to which the nature of God is beyond what we can apprehend by intellect:

> God is greater than all we can say, greater that all that we can know; and not merely does he transcend our language and our knowledge, but he is beyond the comprehension of every mind whatsoever, even of angelic minds, and beyond the being of every substance.[32]

Following Pseudo-Dionysius, in these lines Aquinas holds that God's nature is unknowable, since created and finite beings fall within the realm of our intellect, while God's nature, which is uncreated and infinite, transcends our intellectual capabilities. Then, Aquinas holds that it is impossible to speak properly about God's nature since all the words we may use express a definite manner of being, limited and separated, which is inappropriate for the nature of He in whom all perfections are unified with His essence. Furthermore, our inability to speak truthfully of God's nature is also due to the characteristics of our language, the goal of which is to describe finite things, and thus is not appropriate to describe the infinity of God's nature.

The idea that God's nature is unknowable is found by Aquinas also in the *Liber de Causis*. In the commentary on proposition six of the *Liber de Causis* Aquinas reports with agreement the theory according to which God's nature is unknowable.

> However, the principle which is totally first that is, according to Platonists, the essence of good, is totally unknowable. This is because it does not have anything above itself which can know it. This is the meaning of the word *amethectum*, i. e. what does not exist after another.[33]

---

32   *In Librum Beati Dionysii De divinis nominibus expositio*, I, iii, 77, ed. C. Pera-P. Caramello-C. Mazzantini, Taurini-Romae, 1950. "Deus est potior omni nostra locutione et omni cognitione et non solum excedit nostram locutionem et cognitionem, sed universaliter collocatur super omnem mentem etiam angelicam et super omnem substantiam."

33   *Super Librum De causis*, Prop. VI, 1, VI, 163., ed. H. D. Saffrey, Friburg-Nauwelaerts, Louvain, 1954. "Sed illlud quod est primum simpliciter, quod secundum Platonicos est ipsa essentia bonitatis, est penitus ignotum, quia non habet aliq-

Aquinas shares with the author of the *Liber de Causis* the doctrine that God's nature is unknowable in so far as his nature transcends what is finite: since the proper object of human intellect is what is finite, it is not possible to have any form of knowledge of an object which transcends what is finite. Then, following the author of the *Liber de Causis*, Aquinas indicates that "being" is understood in a different way, when it is said of God and creatures, since when it is said of God, it implies infinite transcendence. The difference lies in the dichotomy between a finite being to which we are proportioned and an infinite being to which we cannot refer. This prevents human beings from reaching God's proper nature through creatures, for the sense in which creatures "are" is radically diverse from the sense in which God "is." Hence, no speech is able to capture God's nature which it is not be rationally attainable by human beings.

As I have already emphasized in the third section, Aquinas's strong intellectualist approach to ethics is grounded in his doctrine of the soul. Aquinas shows, indeed, that the human soul may be considered "divine" for two reasons. First, since its nature is similar, although not identical, with that of separate substances. Second, because the human soul by participation in the intellectual power of God becomes one with him. Aquinas encountered and studied both these doctrines in the *Liber de Causis*, as we can see from his commentary.

The former doctrine occurs in proposition fourteen of the *Liber de Causis*, where the author holds that the human soul is midway between sensible and intelligible things:

> The soul, as was held in proposition 2, is midway between intellectual things, which are altogether separate from motion, and in this are made equal to eternity, and sensible things, which are in motion and fall under time. [...] In this manner all the sensible parts of its body pre-exist virtually in the nature of the soul, for they are adapted to the potencies of the soul, which proceed from its nature. Even though sensible things are in the soul, which is their cause, they are not, however, in it in the manner in which they are themselves. For the power of the soul is immaterial, even though it is the cause of material things, and is spiritual, even though it is the cause of bodies, and is without corporeal dimension, even though it is the cause of things that have dimension.[34]

---

uid supra se quod possit ipsum cognoscere et hoc significat quod dictum *amethectum* idest non post existens alicui."

34  *Super Librum De Causis,* Prop. XIV: "Anima enim, ut habitum est in 2 propositione, media *est inter res intelligibiles quae* sunt omnino separatae a motu et per hoc parificantur aeternitati, *et inter res sensibiles quae moventur* et cadunt sub tempore. [...] Et per hunc modum in natura animae virtute praeexistunt omnes partes sensibiles sui corporis, coaptantur enim potentiis animae quae ex eius natura procedunt. Et quamvis res sensibiles sint in anima quae est causa earum, non tamen sunt in ea per modum quo sunt in seipsis. Nam virtus animae est immaterialis, quamvis sit

Like the author of the *Liber de Causis,* Aquinas suggests that the human soul is half-way between sensible and intellectual beings. For, like intellectual beings, it is without motion, immaterial and spiritual. Nevertheless, it is also similar to sensible beings since it impresses them and directs their activities. Moreover, for the human soul to be related to a body is an intrinsic part of its nature.

The latter doctrine (the participation of the human soul in God's intellectual power) is studied in proposition thirteen where the author of the *Liber de Causis* holds that in every soul there is an identity between the knower and the known object:

> To prove this proposition, the author first states here that in separate intellects *what understands and which is understood are simultaneously* [one thing] inasmuch as they are not only intellects according to their substance but also intelligible as what most closely participate first intellect. So he concludes that *an intelligence understand its essence.* Because its essence is the essence of something that understands, it follows that, by understanding its essence, it understands that understands its essence.[35]

The idea, shared by Aquinas, appears to be that, when the intellect knows, it becomes in a way identical with what it is knowing. Hence, the human intellect when it is involved in the contemplation of God is somehow identical with him.

## Conclusion

In conclusion, Aquinas's theory of contemplation appears to be the result of an extensive dialogue with both the Aristotelian and the Neoplatonic philosophical traditions. More precisely, Aquinas tries to harmonise the Neoplatonic idea that contemplation involves an element that transcends human capacity and the Aristotelian understanding of contemplation as the perfection of human nature. First, on a general level, Aquinas puts forwards a very intellectualist interpretation of Aristotle's ethics. Second, he emphasizes the importance of contemplation, drastically reducing the relevance that political life has in Aristotelian ethics. Finally, through the four steps I analysed in the third section of this paper, Aquinas articulates a theory of contemplation which can be understood as a sort of bridge between Neoplatonic and Aristotelian philosophy.

---

causa materialium, et est spiritualis, quamvis sit causa corporum, et est sine dimensione corporea, quamvis sit causa rerum habentium dimensionem."

35  *Super Librum De Causis,* Prop. XIII 1: "Et ideo ad probandum hanc propositionem, primo hic inducitur quod *intelligens et intellectum* in intellectibus separatis *sunt simul,* in quantum scilicet secundum substantiam suam non solum sunt intellectus sed intelligibiles, utpote propinquissime participantes primum intellectum. Unde concludit quod *intelligentia intelligit essentiam suam.*"

# Aristotle vs. the Neo-Darwinians: Human Nature and the Foundation of Ethics

## Marie I. George

It has been claimed in recent times that a Darwinian theory of human nature provides a basis for a normative ethics. I was initially interested in examining this position as a way of approaching the broader question of what view of human nature will allow for a science of ethics, i.e., for ethical knowledge that would hold good for all times and places. Upon being presented with the conference's question, "Is ethics possible without God?," it occurred to me that it would be interesting to compare the theist philosopher Aristotle and the atheist or agnostic Neo-Darwinians as to whether and how their views about God affect their ability to find a solid anthropological foundation for a science of ethics.

I am not interested here in looking at the *is-ought* question, a common question that arises when someone tries to found ethics on some understanding of human nature. I am going to assume along with Aristotle and the Neo-Darwinians philosophers that human nature is a point of reference which provides a framework for determining non-arbitrary rules for what is right and wrong,[1] without worrying exactly how one gets from the one to the other.

My thesis here is that the most fatal mistakes made in attempts to found ethics lie in misunderstandings concerning nature, both nature in general and human nature. In particular, I think that Aristotle's ethics is a basically sound enterprise because of four positions he holds at the outset. First, in regard to nature, he holds that nature acts for an end. Secondly, in regard to human nature, he holds the following three things: (1) reason is not just another sense power, but is an immaterial faculty capable of grasping goods which are not material; (2) we are truly free; (3) human nature is in some sense fundamentally unchanging. I will argue that Neo-Darwinian attempts to found ethics fail because they deny the above.

I also maintain, however, that one's position concerning the existence of God does have an effect on the foundations of moral science, albeit in a couple

---

1  See Aquinas, *Summa Contra Gentiles*, III, 129, where Aquinas looks to nature to establish that there are things that are naturally right for humans to do.

of less immediate and more subtle ways. I will argue that although one's knowledge of nature is prior to one's knowledge of God's existence, there is a close connection between the question on finality in nature and that of whether there is a Mind behind nature, and for this reason, views on theism and atheism impact upon what respect one thinks should be accorded to nature, and this in turn affects the way one approaches moral questions, for the better or for the worse.

Another point where one's view on God's existence has bearing on the foundations of ethics concerns the existence and nature of the faculties of reason and free will. For it appears that the connection between God's existence and the immaterial nature of reason and free will is such that if one affirms that reason and/or free will are immaterial powers, then one must also affirm that God exists, and if one denies that God exists, one must also deny that immaterial powers in man exist. Given this, I will argue that those Neo-Darwinians who start from atheism as from a first principle cut themselves off from the understanding of human nature requisite for formulating moral science.

### 1. Neo-Darwinian Biology and Neo-Darwinian Philosophy

First, let me clarify the difference between Neo-Darwinian biology and Neo-Darwinian philosophy. Darwinian theory is a biological theory ordered to explaining the diversification of life forms over time. Its central tenet is that the driving forces behind evolution are random variation and natural selection: random variation renders some organisms more reproductively fit, and these "naturally selected" individuals leave more offspring (or at least more genes like their own).[2] Neo-Darwinian theories complete Darwin's picture with knowledge of genetics which explains the sources of variation and how traits are transmitted, and seek to fill in details about the modalities of evolution.

Now a number of thinkers have elaborated philosophical views that take their inspiration from Darwinian biology. Views vary somewhat from one Neo-Darwinian thinker to another, but a commonly held set of core tenets are the following: (1) There are no final causes in nature. Nature does not act for an end. If organisms arise with the necessary parts (and behaviors) to survive and

---

2  According to some biologists, individuals belonging to certain species will sometimes help their parents raise the parents' offspring in place of trying to have their own offspring. A diploid organism shares half its genes in common with both siblings and offspring. Thus, if a diploid organism helps its parents raise a sibling that otherwise would have died, it amounts to the same thing gene-wise as if it had had one offspring of its own. The notion of "inclusive fitness" takes in account both ways in which an organism can pass on genes like its own. See P.J.B. Slater, "Kinship and Altruism," in P. J. B. Slater and T. R. Halliday (eds.), *Behaviour and Evolution* (Cambridge: Cambridge University Press, 1994), 194–200.

reproduce, the production of either the parts in question or the whole organism was in nowise a goal aimed at by the natural agency responsible for their apparition.[3] New features and new organisms arise by chance and the organisms survive if they can meet the environmental challenges they are faced with. (2) Random variation and natural selection adequately account for the adaptations we observe in living nature, and thus remove any need for a supernatural "Designer."[4] Whence Richard Dawkins off-quoted claim that Darwin made it possible to be "an intellectually fulfilled atheist." (3) Human beings are just another animal; as products of the material causes of random mutation and natural selection, we have no immaterial soul and there is no need to appeal to "special creation."[5] (4) In order to understand a given human behavior, one should proceed on the assumption that it, like a behavior belonging to any other animal, is geared to maximizing the passing on of one's own genes, or at least genes similar to one's own.[6]

I in nowise mean to say that if one accepts evolution, and even the Neo-Darwinian account of evolution, one is logically obliged to subscribe to the Neo-Darwinian philosophy just described. I in fact do not think that either is the case, but here is not the place to argue those points. It is simply factually true that this philosophy is espoused by a certain number of those who took their inspiration from a Neo-Darwinian account of evolution.

---

3   George Gaylord Simpson, *The Meaning of Evolution: A Study of the History of Life and of its Significance for Man*, rev. ed. (New Haven, C.T.: Yale University Press, 1967), 344–45: "Although the details remain to be worked out, it is already evident that all the objective phenomena of the history of life can be explained by purely naturalistic or, in a proper sense of the sometimes abused word, materialistic factors. They are readily explicable on the basis of differential reproduction in populations (the main factor in the modern conception of natural selection) and of the mainly random interplay of the known processes of heredity. [...] Man is the result of a purposeless and natural process that did not have him in mind."

4   See Douglas Futuyma, *Evolutionary Biology*, 2nd ed. (Sunderland, Mass.: Sinauer Associates, 1986), 3: "By coupling undirected, purposeless variation to the blind, uncaring process of natural selection Darwin made theological or spiritual explanations of the life processes superfluous."

5   Ernst Mayr, *Towards a New Philosophy of Biology* (Cambridge, Mass.: Harvard University Press, 1988), 193: "Darwin and his followers showed conclusively that man is not a separate creation but the product of common descent."

6   Michael Ruse and Edward O. Wilson, "The Evolution of Ethics," in Michael Ruse (ed.), *Philosophy of Biology* (New York: MacMillan Publishing Company, 1989), 314: "Two propositions appear to have been established beyond any reasonable doubt. First, the social behavior of animals is firmly under the control of genes, and has been shaped into forms that give reproductive advantages. Secondly, humans are animals."

## 2. Does Human Nature Change?

A science of ethics is expected to offer some sort of rules or guidelines for making choices. Those ethicists who reject the idea that these rules are relative to individual desire or relative to the desire of the majority generally turn in one manner or another to human nature as providing an objective basis for what we should and should not do. The basic idea is that just as submersing a blender or putting a spoon in it while it is on is bad for the blender because of the way it is constructed, so too certain activities are good or bad for humans because of the way we are constituted, independent of how we'd like things to be. The question then becomes how are we constituted, so that we can determine what things are good for us to do, and what are not. A doubt looms right away whether the kind of black and white rules for handling a blender can be found in the case of human behavior:

> The subjects studied by political science, the good and the just, involve much difference of opinion and uncertainty, so that they are sometimes believed to be mere conventions and not to exist by nature. And similar uncertainty surrounds the good, because it frequently occurs that good things have harmful consequences: people before now have been undone by wealth, and others by their courage. We must be content, then, in speaking of such subjects and with such premises to indicate the truth roughly and in outline, and in speaking about things which are only for the most part true and with premises of the same kind to reach conclusions that are no better. (Aristotle, *Nicomachean Ethics*, 1094b15–24)[7]

One of the biggest challenges of doing ethics is separating constants in human action from the dizzying variety of circumstances accompanying concrete choices. But what if human nature itself changed? Then there wouldn't be any constants in human action, and morality appropriate in one stage in human history would cease to be so in a later stage. It is in regard to this question that we find one of the biggest differences in traditional ethics and the ethics advocated by many Neo-Darwinian philosophers. I intend to take it up first, followed by the other points of difference, which regard finality in nature, and the existence of free will and of a uniquely human good.

Aristotle appears to weigh in favor of human nature being a changeable nature:

> That justice varies is not absolutely true, but only with qualifications. Among the gods indeed it is perhaps not true at all; but in our world,

---

7   Unless otherwise noted, I am using W. D. Ross' translation of the *Nicomachean Ethics* in Richard McKeon (ed.), *The Basic Works of Aristotle* (New York: Random House, 1968).

> although there is such a thing as natural justice, yet everything is capable of change. But nevertheless there is such a thing as natural justice as well as justice that is not from nature; and it is [not?[8]] clear of things that can be other, which are from nature and which are but legal and conventional, both sorts alike being capable of change. The same distinction holds good in regard to other matters; for instance the right hand is naturally stronger than the left, yet it is possible for any [?all[9]] man to make himself [be born?[10]] ambidextrous. (*NE*, 1134b28–1135a1)

Aristotle here seems to be making more than the innocent claim that human beings are material beings subject to change, looking to the fact that we have a life cycle or that we perfect ourselves through similar choices repeated over a period of time or that the circumstances surrounding our actions are subject to continual flux. The doubts about the text itself make it difficult to get at Aristotle's exact meaning. Certainly, individual humans can be born possessing or lacking features natural to the race (e.g., be born with an extra finger or lacking sight). Still it is hard to see how Aristotle could envisage the entire race changing (in which case what is generally just might have to change).

Aquinas of course comments on this passage,[11] and he speaks about the "mutability of human nature" in regard to the question of justice in other places as well. To quote a passage from the *Summa theologiae*:

> when a being has an unchangeable nature what is natural must always and everywhere be such. The nature of man, however, is changeable. And therefore what is natural to man can be missing. As there is natural equality in rendering a deposit to the one who deposited it, it would be the case that if human nature was always upright this should always be observed. But because it sometimes happens that the will of a person is corrupted, there are cases when the deposit should not be returned, lest a man having a perverse will make bad use of it; as would be the case for instance, if a crazy person or an enemy of the state reclaimed arms that had been left as a deposit.[12]

---

8   See *NE*, trans. H. Rackham (Cambridge, Mass.: Harvard University Press, 1982), 296, suggested emendation of Paley. I have combined Ross's and Rackham's translation.

9   See ibid., omission of "all" suggested by Wilkinson. See also ibid., 294, note b: "The order of the [...] sentences seems confused."

10  See ibid., emendation suggested by Rackham.

11  See *In Decem Libros Ethicorum Aristotelis ad Nicomachum Expositio*, ed. R. M. Spiazzi, O.P. (Turin: Marietti, 1964), nos. 1028, 1029. Hereafter cited as *In Decem Libros Ethicorum Aristotelis*.

12  Aquinas, *ST*, ed. Instituti Studiorum Medievalium Ottaviensis (Ottawa: Commissio Piana, 1953), II-II, q. 57, a. 2, ad 1.

On this account, the need to make an exception to the aforementioned rule of justice does not stem from a change in human nature as such, but from a change in a circumstance, namely, the "to whom." So despite everything that is said by Aristotle and Aquinas regarding the changing character of human nature, they do not appear to mean that human nature changes, but only that the human condition does.

What do the Neo-Darwinians have to say about the changeability of human nature? As David Hull explains:

> One consequence of evolutionary theory is that species as such can have no essences as defined above [namely, a permanent set of necessary and sufficient traits] (Hull, 1965). Rarely if ever can a set of traits be discovered which distinguishes one species from all other species throughout its existence. Species split into two or more species very gradually. At any one time there are species in all states of speciation.[13]

In other words, one might think that a given species X must have a fixed set of traits, say, A, B, and C, and that if an individual is found to have traits A, B, and C it must belong to the species X. The problem Hull is pointing to is that while species X in the beginning had traits A, B, and C, it might with time eventually lose trait A without becoming a new species. And a new species that originated from species X might have traits A, B, and C, plus some other trait that species X lacked.

Ernst Mayr accordingly speaks of species as "temporary incarnations of harmonious, well-integrated gene complexes."[14] He holds that "it is always uncertain whether newly acquired adaptations are of permanent value."[15] This leads Mayr to draw the following conclusions about morality:

> There are two reasons why the traditional norms of the West are no longer adequate. The first is their rigidity. The essence of the evolutionary process is variability and change, and ethical norms must be sufficiently flexible and versatile to be able to cope with a change of conditions. The second reason is that mankind has indeed experienced a drastic accelerating change of conditions. Perhaps the most important component in this change has been the steady enlargement of human groups during the last 10 to 15 thousand years. With the coming of agriculture, a larger group was favored because it could better protect against marauders, and the availability of a good food supply likewise favored population growth. A change in values – for instance, greater emphasis on property rights – was inevitable.

---

13    David Hull, "Are Species Really Individuals?," *Systematic Zoology*, 25 (1976), 174.
14    E. Mayr, *Toward a New Philosophy of Biology* (Cambridge, Mass.: Harvard University Press, 1988), 253.
15    Ibid., 254.

> Some of the ethical norms adopted by the pastoral people of the Near
> East more than 3,000 years ago are altogether inadequate for the modern
> urbanized mass society. [...]
> The third great ethical problem of our day is posed by the discovery of
> our responsibility toward nature as a whole. Growth, whether economic
> growth, populational growth, or whatever other kind of growth, used to
> rank very high in our value system. Even though certain influential people
> [...] have so far failed to appreciate the danger of overpopulation, I cannot
> see how it can be ignored any longer. Certain of our societies, like those of
> China and Singapore, have courageously tackled this problem by a reorder-
> ing of ethical values. The sooner other societies follow, the better it will be
> for the ultimate good of mankind.[16]

Mayr's view that moral values rightly change with the times puts him only
a hairsbreadth from out-and-out relativism – if nature is a measure for him, it is
not a fixed one. And the gap is further narrowed when one takes in account our
ability to manipulate evolutionary pressures placed upon us by the environment,
in addition to which we may eventually perfect ways of altering our very genetic make-up. For example, instead of letting the hole in the ozone layer select for
those individuals more resistant to skin cancer, we make things to protect us
from excess solar radiation, from things as simple as hats to chemical products
such as sun screens. We control our environment in myriad ways, e.g., air conditioning. And through medicine we resist and cure diseases which otherwise
would have eliminated less fit individuals.

### 3. Blind Forces vs. Design

This leads us to a second problem with Neo-Darwinism and ethics. Many Neo-
Darwinian philosophers deny that we should take any cue from our nature in our
decisions to produce technology. According to them, not only is nature inherently changeable, but nothing produced by nature is aimed at. All natural things are
the result of blind forces. Thus, there is no reason to let nature dictate to us what
we should or should not do. From this perspective, it would be ridiculous, for
example, to have moral qualms about in vitro fertilization because it was unnat-
ural. Sure in the olden days humans had to procreate children by a physical act,
and also had to take children as they came. However, now with the advance of
technology babies can be made in a dish, and after tests are done for birth
defects, the parents (or parent) can select the offspring that they (or he or she)
want. Why should a couple having problems conceiving be held back from hav-

---

16   Ibid., 85–87. Ironically, the exact same reasons Mayr gave in 1988 in favor of birth
     control had been explicitly examined twenty years earlier in *Humanae Vitae*, which
     went on to reject them in light of the natural finality of the marital act (see #2).

ing the offspring they desire because of scruples about interfering with natural acts which after all are simply the product of the blind forces random variation and natural selection, and in addition are not written in stone,[17] but may change with time, like any other biological feature. So the Neo-Darwinian attitude that what is natural is merely the product of blind forces further reinforces the notion that a thing's nature in nowise provides a standard for action, a notion derived from their view of natures as being continually open to change. From the Neo-Darwinian perspective, the fact that evolution is a slow process, and thus that human nature is not undergoing radical changes from year to year, ultimately does not argue in favor of a "conservative ethic." Indeed the very slowness of evolution in adjusting a population to changes in the environment is a reason to take things in our own hands. An obvious example of this way of thinking is that given the difficulty the presently large human population has in sustaining itself, why wait for nature to adjust human fertility when one can do so by artificial means.

Aristotle acknowledges a kind of wisdom in nature that the Neo-Darwinians deny.[18] But finally what avail is acknowledging a kind of wisdom in nature vis-à-vis founding moral science, if one concedes that part of the wisdom of nature is that populations/species change in response to environmental changes? Above I noted that those who regard nature to be the product of purely blind causes find in this no reason to respect her.[19] But finally as far as

---

17  See Marc D. Guerra cited by Richard Neuhaus in *First Things* (January 2002), 88: "If there really are no natural limits on human beings, if nature really is in a constant slow rate of flux, how can a Darwinian, even a morally serious Darwinian, oppose something such as the 'new science' of human cloning? A self-conscious Darwinian such as E.O. Wilson realizes that cloning is simply the next state of human 'modification.' Faithful to the spirit of his Darwinism, Wilson looks forward to the day when cloning or 'volitional evolution' will allow scientists to alter 'not just the anatomy and intelligence of the species but also the emotions and creative drive that compose the very core of human nature.'"

18  It would take us too far from my main purpose to point out the weaknesses in the Neo-Darwinian position that blind forces are the sole causes of the adaptations that are present in organisms.

19  It would be a bit of an oversimplification to say that the atheist scientist has no respect for nature. Often these people cannot help feeling awe despite their rejection of anything divine about nature. See, for example, Edward O. Wilson, *The Diversity of Life* (Cambridge, Mass.: Harvard University Press, 1992), 345: "Each species is the product of mutations and recombination's too complex to be grasped by unaided intuition. It was sculpted and burnished by an astronomical number of events in natural selection, which killed off or otherwise blocked from reproduction the vast majority of its member organisms before they completed their lifespans. [...] Such is the ultimate and cryptic truth of every kind of organism. [...] The flower in the crannied wall – it is a miracle. [...] Every kind of organism has reached this moment

looking to nature to provide a fixed standard goes, having a reason to respect nature does not really change matters if one acknowledges that nature is subject to continual change. The evolution of different racial traits is good evidence that our nature is a changeable nature. But is human nature entirely plastic? And to what extent does the changeable character of our nature affect the formulation of unchanging rules for conduct?

### 4. Not Just Animals

Although Aristotle in a certain sense regards our nature as subject to change, in another sense he regards it as fundamentally complete and finished. One fact about human nature, of central importance to the question of how changeable our nature is, is that we are not just animals. Our rational soul is an immaterial substantial form, and reason and free will are immaterial faculties, and as such lie outside the realm of evolutionary processes in nature. As Aristotle puts it, the intellect is "from without."[20] A hybrid of the immaterial and material realm, we possess something of the unchanging quality of the former and something of the changing character of the latter.

Although many evolutionary biologists would deny this, the type of nature that human beings possess is the final point of evolution, which can only go so far as to produce a body suited for an immaterial soul endowed with reason and will. As terminus, it is not surprising that our nature be more fixed than the natures of other organisms. Reason and will are constant features of human nature, whereas wings enabling flight are not constant features of birds, nor are eyes allowing for sight constant features of fish (e.g., cave-dwelling fish have eyes, but lack vision).

The other essential part of human nature is a sensitive body. If a being does not have a sensitive body, it is not human (at least it's not a complete human). But as to the quality of senses and emotions there can be wide variation. As Aristotle points out, however, the senses have no bearing on our moral life to the

---

in time by threading one needle after another, throwing up brilliant artifices to survive and reproduce against nearly impossible odds." And one often finds this strong sense of wonder also among astronomers who are atheists. Moreover, such scientists, especially those in ecology, see that man's failure to respect nature has disastrous consequences for biodiversity, as well as harmful consequences for human life. Ironically, while they will acknowledge that we need to respect the balance of nature, they generally fail to see a need for us to also respect our own nature, and that even greater harm befalls us when we do not do so.

20   See Aristotle, *Generation of Animals*, 736b27–29: "It remains, then that reason alone comes from without and that it alone is divine. For its activity shares nothing with the activity of the body."

extent that that they function well does not generally[21] depend on reason. For example, one doesn't see well because one decides that today one is going to have 20/20 vision. In addition, to the extent that the senses can be directed so as to perceive something in particular, their activity, barring illness, follows immediately upon the command of reason, and thus the moral goodness or badness of the act of sensing commanded accrues to reason alone. For example, the sense of sight is neither good nor bad when one looks at a text of Aristotle or pornography, respectively.[22]

The other essential aspect of the sensitive nature is emotion.[23] If a thing does not have feelings, it is not an animal, for it would be pointless for an animal to be able to perceive food (for example), if it lacked any desire for food.[24] In human beings the emotions have their own motion that is independent of reason, and yet at the same time they are capable of being influenced by reason. For these reasons, the emotions play a role in human goodness or badness. In human beings, the purpose of emotion is to reinforce rational activities.[25] The concupiscible emotions help insure that we nourish ourselves and that the species continue, while the irascible emotions help us avoid and overcome difficulties and dangers.

Underlying our sense abilities are necessarily vegetative functions: nutrition, growth, healing, etc. The sensitive body has to develop to a mature state, replace dead cells, and generate chemicals used up by the activities of sensing and emotion, and these and other like tasks fall to the vegetative part of our soul. The vegetative part of human nature has no bearing on morality. As Aristotle points out, the functioning of this part is automatic,[26] and it, unlike the appetite, in no wise shares in a rational principle by "listening to it and obeying it."[27]

At this point, it is appropriate to add a nuance concerning the question of whether reason can evolve. The faculty of reason, being immaterial, cannot. However, the ability to reason well does in certain indirect ways depend upon the body. Aristotle held that the soul is the substantial form of the body. Whence the soul is going to be affected by the matter it is received into. The same form, when received into marble and into sandstone, is going to result in statues that

---

21  See *NE* 1114a1.

22  See *NE* 1103a26 and *NE* 1106a9.

23  See *NE* 1111b: "The irrational passions do not seem less part of human nature than reason is, and actions proceeding from anger (*thumos*) and desire (*epithumia*) belong to the human being who does them." (Translation mine.)

24  See Aristotle, *De Anima* 414b1–14.

25  See *NE* 1116b30: "Now brave men act for honour's sake, but passion (*thumos*) aids them [...]."

26  See *NE* 1102a33–b5.

27  See *NE* 1102b28.

are different. Aristotle remarks that those who are of "soft flesh" are better
endowed as to intelligence than those of "hard flesh." Without going into the
details of what this "soft flesh" is, it is plain that it is in accord with Aristotelian
views on matter and form that human beings could evolve bodies which would
result in them having more penetrating intellects. The fundamental nature of
reason would not change for so much, as ideas would still be arrived at in the
same manner starting from sense experience.

Whether something similar is true in the case of the will is not easy to say.
We speak of some people having more will-power than others, and perhaps this
is a phenomenon similar to some people being of more penetrating intellect than
others.[28] Aristotle tells us little about the will, and so what he would say about
this matter is not obvious. In any case, the very nature of the will as rational
appetite could not be affected by evolutionary processes.

There is also another way, according to Aristotelian principles, that humans
could become more intelligent.[29] The internal senses that serve reason could in
principle improve through evolution. Thinking depends upon imagining,[30] and
imagination is a brain function. Therefore, in principle the human imagination
could evolve so as to better serve reason. Similarly, future humans might have
better memories, something which would definitely facilitate learning. There
are also natural dispositions of the internal senses that facilitate moral judgments,[31] and these too could, in principle, change for the better or worse across
the species. Again, even if such changes in our ability to reason occurred, the
nature of reason itself would not change.

To summarize: The abilities that belong to human nature that cannot evolve
are reason and will; the ones that can evolve are the vegetative powers, the sense
powers, and the emotions, for these all involve the body, and as such are all subject to change. Among those abilities subject to change, only the emotions have
any essential bearing upon ethics. As for the senses or vegetative powers, even
if they did change, this would not have any impact on the general guidelines proposed by moral science. In a moment I will examine to what extent the emotions

---

28  One might wonder whether the emotions might evolve so as to be more apt to obey
     the rational faculties. It certainly is the case that some people from birth more read-
     ily acquire certain virtues than other people acquire them. (Natural virtue is defined
     later on in the main text.) Improvement from the side of the emotions is limited
     however in the sense that natural virtues always bring with them natural vices. For
     example, a person who is naturally brave is disposed to the vice opposed to meek-
     ness. Thus, while there could be an increase of natural virtue across the population,
     it could never be the case that all the emotions belonging to any given individual be
     naturally well-disposed to following reason.

29  See *ST*, I, q. 85, a. 7.

30  See *De Anima* 431a16: "the soul never thinks without an image."

31  See *NE* 1143b7. See also *ST*, II-II, q. 51, a. 3, ad 1.

are subject to change. But first, I'd like to point out that any evolution of our vegetative powers or senses, while not altering the science of ethics in any way, could have bearing on the morality of our concrete choices.

Imagine that humans evolved the ability to plug their ears with their ear-lobes. Then people would have a moral obligation to plug their ears to prevent themselves from inadvertently eavesdropping on private conversations, just as people under ordinary circumstances have a moral obligation not to read material that has not been addressed to them. The same basic rule of morality regarding privacy would not change with the change in nature; it would simply have broader application than it used to. Or consider, what would obtain if evolution resulted in everyone becoming violently allergic to peanuts. It would then become wrong to consume peanuts because they would affect one's health negatively, and it would be wrong to serve them to others, because this would result in harm to them. Here again the rules of morality would not change. Temperance always requires consuming food so as to stay healthy; hospitality always requires that one serve guests foods that will not make them sick.[32]

When one thinks about it, these fictive scenarios are not much different from real life moral situations, for one always has to take into account the concrete facts. We already have to avoid serving peanuts to the particular individuals who are allergic to them. We already know that it is wrong to serve certain types of mushroom to anyone because they are deadly. It is a universal moral rule that killing innocent people is wrong. However, it pertains to prudence to inform oneself as to which foods are poisonous and which are not. Sometimes it has happened that foods that we initially think are not harmful to health are later discovered to be harmful. But this does not alter the general guidelines that ethics provides for this and like choices,[33] although it does make a difference as to the goodness or badness of a concrete choice. So knowledge about changes in human nature as to vegetative powers or the senses would prove useful for prudential decisions, but would have no impact on the general guidelines for human choices examined in ethics.[34]

---

32   Ruse and Wilson are thus mistaken when they conclude that "Ethics does not have the objective foundation our biology leads us to think it has," on the grounds that: "Natural selection is above all opportunistic. Suppose that, instead of evolving from savannah-dwelling primates, we had evolved in a very different way. If, like the termites, we needed to dwell in darkness, eat each others' faces and cannibalize the dead, our epigenetic rules would be very different from what they are now. Our minds would be strongly prone to extol such acts as beautiful and moral. And we should find it morally disgusting to live in open air, dispose of body waste and bury the dead" ("The Evolution of Ethics," in *Philosophy of Biology*, 317).

33   One does not have to study Ethics to know that killing the innocent is wrong; this is an evident principle of natural law. However, Ethics does reiterate such principles, often going on to draw conclusions from them.

34   See Aquinas, *De Malo*, q. 2, a. 4, ad 13.

### 5. Are Emotions Dispensable Features of Human Nature?

Let us turn now to the questions of whether the concupiscible and irascible appetite could evolve in such a way as to affect ethics. There is plainly a wide variety of emotional dispositions present in the human race. Aristotle was quite aware of this variety, and developed from it his notion of natural virtue and natural vice. Natural virtue and vice are inborn inclinations to moral virtue or vice which follow from the physical make-up proper to the individual.[35] A person's make-up inclines him to feel certain emotions more or less readily, and/or more intensely, and/or more lastingly than other emotions. Some people are naturally fearless while others are born chickens. Some are naturally laid-back, while others are born hot-tempered. The natural virtues and vices of human individuals correspond to a gene pool from which changes in predominant feelings in the human race could in principle arise. But are such changes likely to arise? And if they did, would they cause a reordering of the virtues, or additions or subtractions from the list of virtues that Aristotle speaks of?

Looking at the concupiscible and irascible emotions *grossomodo*, although it is theoretically possible that they be eliminated from the human species, the chances of this happening are for all practical purposes nil. The concupiscible emotion of pleasure is one of the most effective imaginable motivators,[36] contributing greatly to insuring that we maintain our health by eating and that we continue the race by having sex. The pleasure we derive from eating is so widespread in the human race that there in no name for the vice at the other extreme from gluttony, a sign of the natural utility of this emotion.[37]

The emotions of fight or flight are also so conducive to survival, aiding us as they do to overcome or flee danger, that it is hard to imagine any change of environment which would render these emotions non-adaptive. That the human abilities to feel one or the other of these emotions increase or decrease across the race, would not be surprising, but that they be eradicated would. As Aquinas pointed out long ago, humans as a group are a relatively gentle species, for we are social animals, and being overly aggressive is not conducive to living in society.[38] Lowered aggressivity is possibly something that evolved in the human race. And perhaps some change in the natural environment or in society would lead to it (or some other emotional tendency) being increased or decreased across the race. But that the species as a whole change so as to remain entirely unmoved in the face of threats to our lives is not liable to occur, as those

---

35   See *NE* 1109b3–5 and *NE* 1144b3–6.
36   See *NE* 1172a20: "For pleasure seems to be intimately connected with our kind. This is why pleasure and pain are used in educating the young, as means of directing their course." (Translation mine.)
37   See *NE* 1119a5–10.
38   See *In Decem Libros Ethicorum Aristotelis*, n. 1391.

genetically disposed in this manner are likely to lose their lives, and thus are likely to produce fewer offspring, than those individuals lacking such genes.

So what are the chances of temperance and courage as cardinal virtues being phased out of morality? Not very likely given that the emotions they bear upon, pleasure, fear, and anger, are so well suited to help ensure human survival and reproduction. A limited number of individuals may be seriously lacking in these emotions due to natural defect (natural vice), but the spread of such defects across the race would not be favored by natural selection.

If individuals were genetically engineered to entirely lack a certain emotion, the perfection of human nature would be lacking them just as much as, if not more, than if they lacked a limb. Such individuals properly speaking would not be capable of attaining the virtue pertaining to this emotion, although they still could act morally.[39] Consider the fictive case of people who were genetically engineered to be incapable of feeling the emotion of anger. These people nonetheless would be capable of ascertaining an injustice and of moving to fight that injustice, as is appropriate in the circumstances, despite the fact the emotion of anger would not be there to reinforce such activity. The failure of their sense appetite to move in accord with reason is involuntary, and therefore cannot be counted as a moral failing. However, to the extent that the virtue of courage moderates anger (courage chiefly moderates fear and confidence), to that extent these people would be incapable of acquiring or exercising courage. Again, they would also be at a selective disadvantage.

I have considered the concupiscible and irascible emotions in broad outline. Perhaps some of the specific concupiscible and irascible emotions are more

---

39  It is true that the acts of courage and temperance "cannot be of the irascible and concupiscible alone and apart from reason" because "what is more principle in the act of virtue belongs to reason, namely, choice; just as in any operation, the action of the agent is more primary than the passion of what undergoes action" (*Quaestio Disputata De Virtutibus in Communi* in *Quaestiones Disputatae*, vol. 2, ed. P. Bazzi et al. (Turin: Marietti, 1965), unicus, a. 4, ad 2). Still it does not follow from this that one can have acts or habits of temperance and courage in the absence of irascible and concupiscible emotions. Indeed this is why separated substances do not possess these virtues, and why the human soul separated from the body does not possess these virtues: "in the state before the resurrection, the irrational parts will not exist in act in the soul, but will only exist in its essence as rooted in it. [...] Whence, neither will virtues of this sort exist in act, other than in root, namely, in reason and will in which lie certain seeds of these virtues. [...]" (*ST*, I-II, q. 67, a. 1). Thus, only if our hypothetical genetically-engineered anger-less people were physically modified so as to allow them henceforth to feel anger, could they ever perform acts of courage properly speaking, or acquire the virtue of courage (again, to the extent that courage involves anger). See also *Quaestio Disputata De Virtutibus in Communi*, a. 4, ad 13 regarding the need for the appropriate sense appetites (emotions) if one is to possess temperance and courage.

expendable than pleasure, fear, and anger are, though I suspect there is good reason to think that none of them shall disappear from our race. As for new emotions evolving, this is impossible so far as the most fundamental emotions are concerned. Emotions are defined by their objects, which through division we can see to be eleven in number.[40] Emotions other than the basic eleven are a combination of them or a variation of them. Higher animals, i.e., those having some limited sense of the future, manifest all eleven. Humans not only experience the basic eleven, but many added variations of them, due to possessing reason. For instance, animals do not feel envy (sadness at the good of another) or sloth (sadness about spiritual goods).[41]

As for our social nature, this is a consequence of our rational nature.[42] No matter how much improvement evolution brought to our senses, we would always have need of teachers and people to discuss with, for so long as we have an intellect that forms ideas starting from sense experience (which is what it means to have a human intellect), for so long will our minds be like the eye of the bat to the sun when it comes to understanding things most intelligible by nature.[43] So even if other reasons for our coming together in society changed, this reason would always remain.

## 6. The Import of the Unchanging Character of Human Nature for Ethics

Once it is established that reason, will, and the concupiscible and irascible emotions (with the qualification stated) are permanent features of human nature, it becomes clear why morality does not have shifting sand for its foundation.[44] The cardinal virtues which perfect the said parts of the human soul – prudence, justice, temperance and courage – will always be virtues, and acts in accord with them will always lead to human happiness.

---

40  The eleven fundamental emotions are: love and hate, joy and sadness, desire and aversion, hope and despair, fear and confidence, and anger. See *ST*, I-II, q. 23, a. 4.

41  Sloth (*acedia*) is not only in reason, but cannot be felt in beings without reason. See *ST*, II-II, q. 35, a. 3: "Whence if the beginning of a sin lies in sensuality alone, and does not goes so far as to reach the consent of reason, is a venial sin on account of the imperfection of the act. [...] So also the motion of sloth lies sometimes only in sensuality, on account of the struggle of the flesh against the spirit, and this is a venial sin." The same holds true for envy; see *ST*, II-II, q. 36, a. 3.

42  See *ST*, I-II, q. 94, a. 2.

43  This is a paraphrase of Aristotle, *Metaphysics*, 993b10.

44  Put in terms of natural inclinations, evolution would never produce an entire race of humans that did not strive to continue in existence, by seeking nourishment and other life necessities, and by fighting or fleeing dangers. Nor would it produce a human species whose members had no inclination to mate. As for the human inclinations to live in society and know the truth, these are natural to man because of his rationality (see *ST*, I-II, q. 94, a. 2).

In passing, it should be apparent from the above that the idea that we some-how need evolutionary *biology* to provide us with the understanding of human nature for doing ethics is absurd. Aristotle long ago identified which parts of the soul have bearing on morality, along with our basic natural inclinations to live,[45] to form families,[46] to live in society,[47] to know the truth,[48] and so forth. It is a mistake to think that just because some of this knowledge concerns our animal nature, that this means that the ethicist needs to study the science of biology.[49] Most of these things are self-evident, or they are so general that they are objects of philosophical reflection, and not of scientific investigation. Biology can pro-vide us with detailed knowledge useful for making prudential decisions, but not with the sort of general understanding of our nature that is needed for formulat-ing a science of ethics.

The reader has doubtlessly noticed a certain fluidity in the use of the con-cept "human nature." There is an obvious difference between saying that it belongs to human nature to possess free will and that it belongs to human nature to have two feet and the sense of sight. It is impossible for a human being lack-ing free will to exist, but there are people who lack feet and vision. What is absolutely essential to human nature is a rational soul (with all the immaterial faculties that are rooted in this soul) and a sensitive body suited to such a soul.

---

45 See *NE*, 1166a17–20.

46 See *NE*, 1118a8–18: "Of the appetites some seem to be common, others to be pecu-liar to individuals and acquired; e.g., the appetite for food is natural, since every one who is without it craves for food or drink, and sometimes for both, and for the 'mar-riage bed' also, as Homer says, when young and lusty." See also *Politics*, 1252a25–30: "[...] this is a union [i.e., of male and female] which is formed, not of deliberate purpose, but because in common with other animals and with plants, mankind have a natural desire to leave behind them an image of themselves [...]."

47 See *Politics*, 1253a3 and 1253a30–32. See also *NE*, 1169b17.

48 See *Metaphysics,* 98022: "All men by nature desire to know."

49 A good example of how what sociobiologists say may be true, but is not helpful for ethics, is what they say about human "mating strategies." The story is that female animals in view of maximizing the spread of their genes either look to see whether the male is likely to be a good provider, or alternately go for a male that is extreme-ly attractive. The reason for the former strategy is obvious. The latter strategy is based on the notion that if one goes for an attractive male, one will have attractive children; thus what one loses, as far as being provided for goes, is likely to be amply made up for by the greater likelihood that one's children find mates than would less attractive children fathered by the less attractive good provider. Now, first of all, people have observed long ago that some women tend to go for a man because he is wealthy, whereas others take no interest in a man, unless he is a "hunk." We did-n't need sociobiology to tell us that. Nor will women who choose their spouses on such bases be convinced of the error of their ways by taking a crash course in socio-biology.

The organs and bodily abilities that human beings normally have are not essential to human nature, but do pertain to the perfection of the nature.[50] As we have seen, this sort of perfection is relative to the human condition, and is subject to change. So, human nature is both changing and unchanging, but not in the same respect.

Seeing that human nature has an unchanging core to serve as a foundation for a science of ethics does not mean that it is easy to solve all moral problems by reference to human nature. An obvious example of this is in vitro fertilization using the sperm and ovum of a married couple having fertility problems, with the embryo being implanted in the said woman (assume for the moment that all embryos created were implanted). Would Aristotle regard this as art helping nature doing what she intended, or as the generation of offspring in a manner contrary to the way nature intended?

## 7. Morality without Freedom or Moral Goods?

I will turn now to another problem with the Neo-Darwinian understanding of human nature vis-à-vis formulating an ethics, namely, its denial of free will. If ultimately we are determined by material factors, freedom is an illusion. And in fact a certain number of evolutionary biologists are quite comfortable with this view.[51] Granted that freedom, responsibility, self-control are not things that are first and foremost known through observation, scientific or other, this does not mean that they are unknown. Rather they are known with great certitude through one's internal experience – as any child knows when he starts using the expression: "I didn't mean it; it was an accident!" A materialist philosophy rejects a priori anything which is not a property or manifestation of matter. Yet my internal experience of my behavior is that I am not controlled by material factors; I am capable of self-control. I can override both genetic propensities and conditioning, albeit often only with difficulty and with less than perfect consistency. And I feel ashamed even without being caught when I know that what I did was unreasonable and that I did not have to do it. If what I do is the result of material causes, there is no room for the moral "should" or for true shame. I do what I have to do. And so morality goes out the window.

Yet another obstacle that Neo-Darwinian materialists run up against in laying out groundwork for morality springs from their view that human beings are just animals whose goals are identical with those of any other animal. Success for an animal in the first instance means survival, but survival is only a means to the ultimate goal of reproduction, of spreading one's genes. If human are just

---

50   See *ST*, I-II, q. 18, a. 1.
51   See for example, William Provine, "Evolution and the Foundation of Ethics," in *MBL Science*, 3, 1, (Winter 1988), 25–29.

animals, this would be our goal as well. But one of the first things that one has to understand about ethical action is that its goal is not first and foremost survival and reproduction. The goal of a human life is not just to live, but to live in accord with reason. To save one's own life by taking another's life preserver is a manifestly immoral act.

Or so you would think. Actually some evolutionary thinkers in the past were of another opinion. They advocated the active and/or passive elimination of people who were not immediate threats upon their life, such as the handicapped and the mentally retarded.[52] After all, these relatively unproductive individuals are using up resources, and to make matters worse are liable in some cases to produce offspring like themselves.[53] Appealing to the concept of human dignity is of out of the question. The materialist biologists in question reject this concept. An amoeba is just as good as a person.[54] Of course, not all evolutionary biologists of a materialist stamp endorse eugenics, and nowadays many explicitly distance themselves from it. However, one can question whether they are being consistent with their principles. For if social consensus allowed one to engage in such a practice without social repercussions that would reduce one's fitness more than euthanizing "competitors" would increase it, then it seems according to Darwinian principles that one should engage in it.

Regardless of what Neo-Darwinian philosophers think about eugenics, they fail to ascribe a uniquely human good to man, but assign to him the same goods that one would assign to any animal: life, health, pleasure, offspring, and external goods conducive to the things just named. It is a little hard to get ethics off the ground if the "goods of the soul" are reduced to mere sentiment; if the moral good is not even on the list of things to be sought.

## 8. Ethics without God?

It is time to ask what God has to do with ethics. Does Aristotle call upon God in formulating ethical teachings? Certainly, he thinks that God exists, as one can see from his argument that starts from motion in nature and concludes to the unmoved mover. He mentions God (or the gods) a number of times in the *Nicomachean Ethics*, e.g., he says:

---

52  Herbert Spencer and Sir Richard Galton are perhaps the best-known advocates of eugenics who take inspiration from Darwin.

53  The basic notion behind eugenics had already been enunciated by Darwin himself: "The weak members of civilized societies propagate their kind. No one who has attended to the breeding of domestic animals will doubt that this must be highly injurious to the race of men" (Darwin, *The Descent of Man* (New York: The Modern Library, 1962), 501). Note that despite this observation, Darwin rejected eugenics.

54  See Ruse and Wilson, "The Evolution of Ethics," in *Philosophy of Biology*, 313.

And so too, it seems, should one make a return to those with whom one has studied philosophy; for their worth cannot be measured against money, and they can get no honor which will balance their services, but still it is perhaps enough, as it is with the gods and with one's parents, to give them what one can. (*NE*, 1164b2–5)

However, Aristotle derives the fundamental concept upon which the entire *Ethics* is based without making any reference to God,[55] but rather by looking to human nature.[56] The concept in question, of course, is happiness.[57]

Still I would not go so far as to say that Aristotle's theism had no bearing on the success of his ethics. An important difference in the way Aristotle and the Neo-Darwinians approach ethics is that while Aristotle recognizes a certain wisdom in nature, the Neo-Darwinian philosophers regard it as the product of blind forces. This engenders a respect for nature on the part of Aristotle, that is absent in the Neo-Darwinians. I think that a case can be made that Aristotle goes a step further, to reason from the wisdom in nature to the wisdom behind nature. Once having recognized the divine wisdom behind nature, Aristotle is able to turn around and regard nature as a product of the divine, and this engenders even greater respect for nature.

It is true that Aristotle in the *Physics* never reasons to a Mind behind nature the way that he reasons to the Unmoved Mover. However, Aristotle is quite aware that the activities of plants and the instinctive behavior of animals are for the sake of something, and that these beings lack the ability to figure out for themselves the appropriate means that they adopt to their ends. How could Aristotle adamantly reject the chance-necessity explanation for the origin of the adaptive characteristics of such organisms, and yet not see that a complete

---

55   It has been argued that the notion of God is needed to establish that there is an ultimate end for man, because a key principle in the argument for an ultimate end is that all desire cannot be in vain (see *NE*, 1094a22), and the notion that nature does nothing in vain can only be understood by bringing in the notion of God. While a full understanding of "nature does nothing in vain" does require bringing in God, this principle can nonetheless be understood simply by induction, e.g., nature does not give wings to dolphins, or fins to birds, etc.

56   See *NE*, 1097b23–1098a18.

57   Aristotle's next major discussion concerns virtue. He begins by noting: "By human virtue we mean not that of the body but that of the soul; and happiness also we call an activity of soul. But if this is so, clearly the student of politics must know somehow the facts about the soul, as the man who is to heal the eyes or the body as a whole, must know about the eyes or the body" (*NE*, 1102a15–19). Aristotle then proceeds to give a division of the parts of the soul drawn from natural philosophy, and uses this as the basis for distinguishing the main types of virtue (see *NE*, 1102b34–1103a5). Later in Bk. VI, which concerns intellectual virtue, Aristotle again looks first at what is known about the parts of the human soul, before he goes on to investigate the virtues that perfect those parts (see *NE*, 1139a1–16).

explanation requires positing a Mind capable of ordering things to their end? A second reason for thinking that he reasoned to a Mind behind nature is that in the *Nicomachean Ethics* he says:

> Indeed it is possible that in reality people do not pursue the pleasure they think and would say they do, but all pursue the same pleasure. For all things of nature have something of the divine.[58] (*NE*, 1153b30–32)

Aristotle appears to be saying here that God is the author of the ordering to an end present in natural things.[59]

Recognizing that nature is a product of divine art does not automatically engender respect for it, but it certainly is apt to do so. And judging from Aristotle's oft-quoted protreptic in the *Parts of Animals* about the gods in the kitchen,[60] it is reasonable to think that he did have a deep respect for nature as a work of God.

The counterpart of Aristotle's reasoning from finality to God, to a greater respect for nature is found on the part of the Neo-Darwinians. Those that do not start out with atheism as a fundamental assumption, start from what they regard as the sufficiency of blind forces to account for the adaptations that are observed

---

58 There is another more obscure statement which appears to make a similar point in the *Nicomachean Ethics*: "But perhaps even in inferior creatures there is some natural good stronger than themselves which aims at their proper good" (*NE*, 1173a4).

59 Aquinas concurs with this reading. He takes Aristotle to be saying that: "all men desire the same pleasure according to natural appetite, but not nevertheless according to their own judgement. For not all think in their heart or state orally that the same pleasure is the best. Nevertheless all are naturally inclined to the same pleasure as the best, to wit in the contemplation of the intelligible truth, according as all men naturally desire to know. And this happens because all have in themselves something divine, namely, the inclination of nature which depends upon the first principle; or also the form itself which is the principle of this inclination" (*In Decem Libros Ethicorum Aristotelis*, n. 1511). There are other reasons for thinking that Aristotle reasoned to God as the Mind behind nature, for example, as I already mentioned, he maintains that "God and nature do nothing in vain" (*De Caelo*, 271a33). As for the position that Aristotle does not regard God as the efficient cause of the order in nature, Aquinas for one explicitly rejects it: "It is to be noted that Aristotle here posits God to be the maker of the heavenly bodies, and not only a cause through the mode of the end, as certain were saying" (*In Libros Aristotelis De Caelo et Mundo*, Leonine edition (Rome: Society for the Propagation of the Faith, 1886) Bk. I, chap. 4, lectio 8, n. 14, 36).

60 See *Parts of Animals*, 645a17–23: "[I]n all natural things there is something of the wonderful. As it is told about the strangers who wishing to see Heraclitus, hesitated when they saw him at the kitchen warming himself at the stove – Heraclitus bid them not to fear entering, for there are gods even here, so too we should venture on the study of every kind of animal without distaste; for in all of them is something natural and beautiful." (Translation mine.)

in living things. They then reason that since design (or adaptations) in organisms provided up until Darwin's day the basis for the strongest case in favor of God's existence, now that random variation and natural selection adequately explain design, there is far less reason to think that God exists. (The fact that the design argument is not the only argument for the existence of God explains why some Neo-Darwinians are agnostic, rather than atheist). Once the Neo-Darwinians have gone from blind forces in nature to atheism, their atheism tends to reinforce their lack of respect for nature.

Let us go back now to the Neo-Darwinian rejection of the moral good and of free will. Is this a consequence of their atheism, such that if they ceased to deny the existence of God, they would necessarily recognize that man has certain immaterial abilities? The situation is somewhat complex as there are at least two camps among the Neo-Darwinians on this point. Some Neo-Darwinians, following in the footsteps of Darwin himself,[61] do not exclude the existence of non-material entities (God and other) as their very starting point, but end up rejecting them because blind forces seem adequate to explaining the way things are. These thinkers see both God and the immaterial aspects of man to be eliminated by random variation and natural selection. Their atheism is not the cause of their rejection of any immaterial aspect to man.

In the case of other Neo-Darwinians, however, their affirmation of materialism is in direct function of their desire to rid the world of supernatural explanations. As the biologist Richard Lewontin puts it:

> We have a prior commitment, a commitment to materialism. It is not that the methods and institutions of science somehow compel us to accept a material explanation of the phenomenal world, but, on the contrary, that we are forced by our a priori adherence to material causes to create an apparatus of investigation and a set of concepts that produce material explanations, no matter how counterintuitive, no matter how mystifying to the uninitiated. Moreover, that materialism is absolute, for we cannot allow a Divine Foot in the Door.[62]

---

61   Darwin started out a theist and a great admirer of Paley. It was the apparent success of explanation of biological adaptations in terms of material causes alone that led to his questioning God's existence: "The old argument of design in nature, as given by Paley, which formerly seemed to me so conclusive, fails, now that the law of natural selection has been discovered. We can no longer argue that, for instance, the beautiful hinge of a bivalve shell must have been made by an intelligent being, like the hinge of a door by man. There seems to be no more design in the variability of organic beings and in the action of natural selection, than in the course which the wind blows." Darwin, *Autobiography*, quoted by Mayr, *Towards a New Philosophy of Biology*, 239.

62   Richard Lewontin, *New York Review of Books* (January 9, 1997), 31.

This position is an agenda,[63] rather than a work of reason; it proceeds from the way one wants things to be instead of from what is known. So, in a way, it is not even worthy of refutation. It is an extremely influential agenda, however. Moreover, there does seem to be an element of truth in what Neo-Darwinians like Lewontin say, to the extent that although one does not discover the immaterial nature of reason and will as a kind of deduction from the existence of God, such immaterial faculties could not exist if there were no God. So, if one acknowledged that such immaterial faculties existed, then the Divine Foot would be in the Door, for it seems that one would have to also acknowledge that God existed – albeit thinkers such as Aristotle and Aquinas never proposed an argument for the existence of God taken from the immateriality of the human soul.

Materialism is always destructive of the notions that man has knowledge of non-sensible goods and is truly free,[64] but it is not always derived from atheism. Thus one cannot say without qualification that the way to recuperate the kind of understanding of human nature required for ethics is to put God into the picture. It is true, however, that denying God's existence as a first principle necessarily entails the rejection of the intelligible good and of free will. Unless one could change Lewontin and company's minds about God's existence, there is no possibility that they found a sound ethics. However, even if one did change their mind, this would not of itself convince them of the true nature of reason and free will, but would only make them open to reconsidering their "counterintuitive" explanations of human nature and behavior.

While I do not think that there is as much reason to lament an ethics without God, as an ethics without a proper understanding of nature, there are reasons to think that there has to be at least openness to the possibility that God exists, if ethics is going to get on its feet; and this for two reasons. Ethics as a science formulated by natural reason finds its immediate foundation in nature, and thus mistakes about the nature of human reason, of human freedom, and of the changing-ness of human nature have fatal consequences for the development of a sound ethics. Now, the denial of God's existence seems to entail the denial of

---

63  See ibid., 28: "[T]he primary problem is not to provide the public with the knowledge of how far it is to the nearest star and what genes are made of, for that vast project is, in its entirety, hopeless. Rather, the problem is to get them to reject irrational and supernatural explanations of the world, the demons that exist only in their imaginations, and to accept a social and intellectual apparatus, Science, as the only begetter of truth."

64  Materialists come in many flavors, and doubtlessly some of them *claim* that their materialism leaves room for free will, as, for instance, is the case of those who regard free will as an emergent property and/or who adopt certain versions of non-reductive materialism. The latter could formulate a science of ethics in their ignorance that they have undermined one of the very foundations of ethics.

the existence of any less perfect immaterial entity, including reason and free will, whence moral science is gutted. The denial of immaterial faculties in man also subtracts the reason for maintaining that human nature is fundamentally unchanging, whence moral science is destroyed twice over. The other way in which denial of God's existence undermines ethical science is by making it very difficult, if not impossible, to maintain that nature acts for an end or, in other words, that that there is a kind of intelligence in the workings of nature which needs to be respected. The efforts of the person seeking to formulate a science of ethics in the absence of an attitude of respect towards nature are doomed to limited success. I am not saying that one needs to affirm that God exists in order to recognize that there is finality in nature. Indeed, I think the latter is more manifest, and a reason for concluding the former. However, one must be at least open to the possibility that God exists. And it is the person who does recognize a Mind behind nature as being the ultimate cause of the wisdom in nature who is best disposed to a full and proper appreciation of that wisdom. The attitude that we cannot let nature dictate to us what we should do is plainly at cross-purposes with trying to found ethics on an understanding of human nature.[65] "Ethics without God," then, meaning that a denial of God's existence is presupposed to the formulation of an ethics is far more problematic than "Ethics without God" meaning that no explicit reference to God's existence is made.[66]

---

65  Here is an example illustrating how difference in attitude towards nature impacts on moral science: Aristotle would never countenance same-sex marriages, whereas Neo-Darwinians would be inclined to say that "we should not let nature dictate to us how we should behave, times have changed and our overpopulated planet is not indeed of additional members."

66  It would be interesting to consider how faith in God would impact on the formulation of a science of ethics. However, space does not allow us to pursue this classic question regarding the relation of faith and reason.

# The Metaphysical Presuppositions of Natural Law in Thomas Aquinas: A New Look at Some Old Questions

## Anthony J. Lisska

### Introduction

The role of philosophical anthropology in the moral theory of Thomas Aquinas is a hotly debated issue in contemporary Aquinas studies. Proponents of what has been called "the New Natural Law" – John Finnis, Germain Grisez, Robert George, *et alia* – argue that an analysis of practical reason without an ontological foundation in terms of a philosophical anthropology is sufficient in order to develop a theory of natural law fully compatible with the insights of Aquinas. Other philosophers question this method of analysis on the texts of Aquinas.

This essay probes the metaphysical underpinnings of Aquinas's moral theory. The argument articulated is that Aquinas's moral theory is a second order inquiry based squarely on the metaphysical foundations of his theory of the human person, which in turn is rooted in his natural kind ontology. Hence, this essay is an inquiry into the metaphysical presuppositions of Aquinas's natural law theory. The analysis put forward in this essay is a "new look" at some "old questions" in natural law theory. The philosophical queries to be considered are the following:

1. How does the concept of "natural kind" fit into contemporary discussions in philosophy?

2. From a theory of natural kinds as foundational for moral theory, is it possible to transcend the limits of the naturalistic fallacy?

3  Is it possible to develop an adequate theory of obligation within the context of a foundational natural kind ontology?

4  Do the metaphysical presuppositions of natural law theory necessarily lead to the existence of God?

The architectonic of this essay is a response to these four queries. First, in opposition to analytic philosophers like Myles Burnyeat,[1] a persuasive dialectic for natural kind theory based on Aquinas's analysis of form is possible. The ontological possibility of form depends upon an analysis of synthetic a priori causal properties. For Aquinas, these causal properties are dispositional in character. Hence, Aquinas's natural kind ontology is grounded in dispositional properties. Secondly, if one takes these synthetic necessary properties fundamentally as dispositional in mode, one has a method for transcending the limits of G. E. Moore's naturalistic fallacy.[2] Thirdly, using what R.-A. Gauthier once called "the metaphysics of finality," one can develop a theory of obligation based upon a dispositional theory of human nature. Lastly, one must distinguish between an ontology of natural kinds and an ontology entailing divine existence. The scope of these final two questions – a theory of obligation and the existence of God – is distinct.

A central metaphysical question entails an analysis of substantial form as a necessary condition for establishing synthetic necessary properties, which are dispositional in structure. This dispositional analysis in turn is a necessary condition for defending ethical naturalism in Aquinas. Furthermore, this analysis proposes a theory of obligation dependent on a natural kind ontology. This essay stresses that a metaphysical inquiry into natural kind ontology is a necessary condition for rendering Aquinas's moral theory coherent and, furthermore, is independent conceptually from a direct first order relation to the existence of God.

### The Role of Metaphysics

In discussing the role of metaphysics in Aquinas and in natural law theory, several distinctions must be discussed. The foil is the denial of the necessity of a philosophical anthropology as a necessary condition for explicating Aquinas on natural law. Some Thomist critics of the New Natural Law approach of Finnis/Grisez adopt a particular metaphysical/theological paradigm and argue that this scheme is a necessary condition for underpinning natural law theory in Aquinas. Others deny this entailment of a proposition requiring God's existence. Hence, in considering metaphysics as necessary for natural law in Aquinas – and thus offering a critical response to Finnis/Grisez – at least two versions of metaphysical inquiry require discussion.

    a. *"Theological" Metaphysics* (for want of a better term):
    Some Thomist critics of Finnis/Grisez like Steven Long and Fulvio Di
    Blasi, among others, wish to defend the position that the only type of

---

1    M. F. Burnyeat, "Is An Aristotelian Philosophy of Mind Still Credible?" in Martha Nussbaum and Amelie Oksenberg Rorty, editors, *Essays on Aristotle's De Anima* (Oxford: The Clarendon Press, 1992, 1995), pp. 15–26.

2    G. E. Moore, *Principia Ethica* (Cambridge: Cambridge University Press, 1903).

metaphysics found in Aquinas concludes to the position that God is a necessary condition for understanding natural law.[3] It may be the case that one is forced into a position of natural theology after considering the finite character of human beings. However, this theological/metaphysical position concludes to a stronger position. Without God, this position affirms, a consistent account of the metaphysical and moral foundation of natural law in Aquinas is impossible.

b. *Natural Kind Metaphysics:*
An alternative metaphysical theory argues that the existence of natural kinds – essences in Thomas – is a self-sufficient ontological inquiry. Aquinas is at least doing this in his metaphysical discussions. In other words, what is necessary for an adequate metaphysical underpinning for natural law in Aquinas is a theory of natural kinds. The question regarding a dependency-relation to God is a second order question, which follows only after the question of natural kinds has been resolved.

This distinction of two versions of a metaphysical theory and its consequences in Aquinas is necessary for this analysis. In responding to Position (a) above, one might argue that the theological/metaphysical critics have begged the question on the nature of metaphysical inquiry. Thomist critics of the new natural law theory need to recall that a natural law philosopher like Henry Veatch argued that a self-sufficient ontological position on human nature was sufficient for articulating a theory of natural law. Veatch elucidated a consistent theory of natural law using properties of human nature as the foundation for this theory. In his *Rational Man*, Veatch wrote: "I wish to set forth a book on ethics, ethics without religion, if you will."[4] Veatch occupies a middle ground between the Finnis/Grisez "New Natural Law" position and the Thomist metaphysical/theological position defended by Long and Di Blasi. Hence, the ontological work of Veatch is important in these discussions.[5] Articulating the role of ethical naturalism derived from human nature itself is in itself a valuable philosophical investigation; moreover, it is compatible with the moral philosophy of Thomas.

---

3   Steven Long, "Natural Law or Autonomous Practical Reason: Problems for the New Natural Law Theory," in John Goyette, Mark S. Latkovic, and Richard S. Myers: *St. Thomas Aquinas and the Natural Law Tradition: Contemporary Philosophical and Theological Perspectives* (Washington, DC: Catholic University of America Press, 2004); Fulvio Di Blasi, *God and the Natural Law: A Rereading of Thomas Aquinas* (Notre Dame, IN: St. Augustine Press, 2006).

4   Henry Veatch, *Rational Man* (Indianapolis, IN: The Liberty Fund, 2003), p. xxvii.

5   Additional works of Henry Veatch include *For an Ontology of Morals* (Evanston, IL: Northwestern University Press, 1973) and *Human Rights: Fact or Fancy?* (Baton Rouge, LA: Louisiana State University Press, 1985), among others.

### Burnyeat on Incomprehensibility of Form in Aquinas: A Problem

For St. Thomas, a theory of essence depends on a theory of substantial form. Among several recent critiques of the concept of form in Aristotelian philosophy, one of the more widely read is Myles Burnyeat's "Is An Aristotelian Philosophy of Mind Still Credible?" in which Burnyeat argued that Aristotelian ontology is not credible, and moreover "ought to be junked."[6] This wholesale "junking" applies equally to Aquinas's moral theory insofar as natural law depends on a theory of essence that is based on substantial form. Burnyeat bases his conclusions on modern philosophy's dismissal of Aristotelian hylomorphism. According to Burnyeat, modern philosophy, riding on the coattails of the rise of the new science with its theory of corpuscular matter, rejected unequivocally any theoretical significance for matter and form put forward in medieval philosophy. Matter was no longer the "enformed" matter characteristic of medieval Aristotelianism. The demise of matter/form ontology entails the rejection of ethical naturalism in Thomas, since ethical naturalism depends foundationally on some acceptance of matter and form as necessary for an Aristotelian essence. Simply put, Burnyeat argued that a theory of ontological hylomorphism is neither acceptable nor understandable by contemporary philosophers.[7]

One might offer two rejoinders to what Burnyeat affirmed concerning the rejection of a philosophical theory of form in analytic philosophy. Both rejoinders suggest that contemporary ontology must consider the issue of the formal structures of reality. The first response to Burnyeat, developed in some detail below, is drawn from the writings of Everett J. Nelson, with special emphasis on his "The Metaphysical Presuppositions of Induction."[8] Nelson argues that sci-

---

6    M. F. Burnyeat, *op. cit.*

7    Burnyeat's philosophy of mind also appears to argue against what he took to be the materialist/physicalist account of Aristotle put forward by Richard Sorabji in "Intentionality and Physiological Processes: Aristotle's Theory of Sense-Perception," in Nussbaum and Rorty, pp. 195–225. Martha Nussbaum and Hilary Putnam wrote an extensive response to the Burnyeat challenge to Aristotle's philosophy of mind. In essence, they refute the materialist account put forward by Sorabji and offer a modified functionalist account of Aristotle. In this author's judgment, all three philosophers neglected a theory of intentionality. It is by intentionality theory that Aristotle and Aquinas find a middle ground between Cartesian dualism on the one hand and the physicalism of many contemporary studies in the philosophy of mind on the other. These issues in the philosophy of mind and intentionality theory, however, are beyond this discussion of ethical naturalism in Thomas Aquinas.

8    Presidential address delivered at the Sixty-fifth Annual Meeting of the Western Division of the American Philosophical Association, and printed in the *Proceedings and Addresses of the American Philosophical Association: 1996–1968* (Yellow Springs, OH., 1967), pp. 19–33; reprinted in Anthony J. Lisska, *Philosophy Matters* (Columbus: Merrill, 1977), pp. 249–60.

entific laws require synthetic necessary (*a priori*) categories of causality and substance. What Nelson proposes is similar structurally to the Aristotelian concepts of formal cause and primary substance found in the writings of Aquinas. Hence, matter is "structured" in a formal way.

The second response, only briefly sketched here because of space limitations, comes from the recent work of Hilary Putnam[9] and John Haldane.[10] Both Putnam and Haldane suggest that the model of efficient causality prominent in early modern philosophy – and adopted in principle by Burnyeat with his rejection of matter/form ontology – fails to provide an adequate foundation for perception theory in the philosophy of mind. Haldane argues that what contemporary philosophy of mind requires is a return to the Aristotelian hylomorphism found in the writings of Thomas. Haldane writes: "I will proceed boldly and suggest that progress (in the philosophy of mind) may be achieved by making use of the ancient doctrine of hylomorphism."[11] Haldane argues that "formal identity" between mind and thing is a necessary condition in order for awareness to be "veridical" in any significant sense of the term. Therefore, the philosophical dialectic Haldane proposes requires some account of form in order for a theory of perception to cohere theoretically. A discussion of matter/form ontology articulated in the writings of Aquinas, therefore, offers important insights for several issues discussed in contemporary analytic philosophy.

Burnyeat's rejection of Aristotelian ontology theory based on his analysis that modern theories of matter entail the rejection of form will not pass muster in either contemporary metaphysics or philosophy of mind. Insofar as Nelson and Putnam/Haldane argue for the necessity of "enformed" matter, both offer rejoinders to Burnyeat's thesis. Therefore, since substantial form is a necessary condition for developing a theory of natural kinds, and since Thomas's ethical naturalism in his natural law theory is dependent upon a concept of natural kinds, it follows that the establishment of the ontological necessity for form is a necessary condition for undertaking a justification of ethical naturalism.

**Everett J. Nelson and Synthetic Necessary Properties: A Realist Ontology**

One way of reestablishing the importance of substantial form in contemporary metaphysical discussions is through an analysis of Nelson's arguments postulating

---

9   Hilary Putnam, "Aristotle's Mind and the Contemporary Mind;" p. 29. John Haldane kindly shared an unpublished manuscript. The essay has since appeared in *Aristotle and Contemporary Science*, eds. Demetra Sfendoni-Mentzou, Jagdish Hattiangadi, and David M. Johnson (New York: Peter Lang, 2000), vol. 1, pp. 7–28.

10  John Haldane, "A Return to Form in the Philosophy of Mind," in *Form and Matter: Themes in Contemporary Metaphysics*, edited by David S. Oderberg (Oxford: Blackwell Publishers, 1999), p. 54.

11  Haldane, *op. cit.*, p. 41.

the necessity of synthetic necessary causal properties. This work is propaedeutic towards establishing a theory of natural kinds.

In opposition to the prevalent "event ontologies" proposed in early analytic philosophy by Russell and Ayer, among others, Nelson argued for an ontology rooted in substance. These substances, moreover, had synthetic necessary causal connections between them that justified inductive knowledge. In his "The Relation of Logic to Metaphysics," Nelson argued that "…a function of philosophy is to reveal the presuppositions of our beliefs about the world and to construct a hypothesis which satisfies these presuppositions and interrelates those to all fields of knowledge."[12] In his American Philosophical Association Presidential address, Nelson asked the following question important for any realist ontology: "Just what must the principle of induction assert about *the formal structure of the world* in order that it and the empirical data, taken together, would entail the likelihood of the conclusion?"[13] Nelson argued that a justified principle of induction requires as a necessary condition "…the truth of some non-empirical principle that entails that the world or course of events embodies a type of unity that can ground laws and such that instances of them are evidence for them."[14] The realist thrust of Nelson's ontology is readily apparent. He proposed formal structures to reality, a metaphysical claim denied by Burnyeat.

## Nomic and Accidental Universal Propositions

Nelson postulated real connections of causality in order to justify what he took to be the real distinction between "nomic universal propositions" and "accidental universal propositions." A nomic universal proposition would be a genuine law-like statement. An accidental universal proposition would be a general statement based on a property that does not generate a law-like proposition.

Examples of nomic universal propositions would be the following:
a. "An acid and a base yield a soluble salt and water."
b. "All humans are mortal."
c. "All crows are black."

Examples of accidental universal statements would be the following:
a. "All the new buildings on the Notre Dame campus are beige brick."
b. "All the chairs in this room are blue."
c. "All Yuppies drive Sport Utility Vehicles and talk incessantly on cell phones while driving."

12   *The Philosophical Review*, Vol. LVIII, # 1 (January, 1949), p. 1.
13   Nelson, "The Metaphysical Presuppositions of Induction," found in Lisska, p. 256 (italics not in the original).
14   Nelson, *Ibid.*

According to Nelson, only a nomic universal proposition will hold under the scrutiny of a "contrary to fact" or "subjunctive conditional" statement. For instance, one might state categorically: "*Were* this an acid and a base, it *would* yield a soluble salt and water." Under normal conditions, one cannot imagine an instance in chemistry when an acid and a base would not yield a soluble salt and water. An acid and a base are connected causally in virtue of what their predicates signify *in rerum natura*.

Conversely, the same contrary to fact or subjunctive conditional will *not* hold for an accidental universal proposition: "Were there a chair in this room, it would necessarily be blue." The subjunctive conditional does not hold in this case because there is nothing about being a chair in this room that necessitates that it be blue. It might be brown, purple, red, green, or whatever. A Franciscan Missionary of Mary in Northern Alaska might own a SUV and use a cell phone in order to make her ministry rounds in the winter season over the frozen tundra; one would hardly call her a "Yuppie"! One can disconfirm easily any accidental universal proposition. A contrary to fact conditional, however, will hold for nomic universal propositions. Nelson argued that this real, categorical distinction and ontological difference must be justified.[15]

## Synthetic Necessary Connections in the World.

Nelson proposed that the distinction between nomic and accidental universal propositions can be affirmed only if some ontological categories are true of the world. The connection between an acid and a base, for instance, is more than an accidental grouping of properties. It is not, so Nelson argues, merely a randomly assembled class of properties or a "heap" of qualities. The connection, moreover, is not reducible to an analytic proposition, because the causal connection between an acid and a base does not depend on the use of language. The category of cause is not reducible to a linguistic or conceptual connection. Nelson's account is similar to what Saul Kripke, in *Naming and Necessity*, among other places, once called the "metaphysically necessary."[16] Kripke calls the "metaphysically necessary" a truth that is dependent on reality. This concept is not a mere convention of human language. Hence, the "metaphysically necessary" is not coextensive with the semantic notion of "analytic necessity" common in

---

15   Nelson reminds one of Aristotle's *Categories* [1b] where Aristotle affirms the distinction between properties "said of" and properties "found in" primary substances. Properties "said of" are reducible to nomic universal statements; these are the sets of essential or sortal properties that determine a natural kind. On the other hand, properties "found in" are reducible to accidental universal properties. These accidental properties do not determine the essence of the thing but are related, as Aquinas would say, in a *per accidens* manner to the individual.

16   Saul Kripke, "Identity and Necessity," in *Identity and Individuation*, edited by Milton K. Muniz (New York: New York University Press, 1971), pp. 144–46.

English speaking philosophy since Hume. Kripke suggests that the proposition, "Water is $H_2O$," is a metaphysically necessary truth because something would not be water if it were not $H_2O$. This is the essence, or what Kripke calls the "natural kind" of water. This structure is the nature of the kind of thing water is, and it is, Kripke argues, true in all possible worlds. Kripke's concept of the metaphysically necessary is commensurate with what Aquinas holds for a substantial form. For Aquinas, like Aristotle, an account of an essence is more than a modal necessity. Aquinas intends a *de re* (about things) necessity and not a *de dicto* (about language) necessity. This *de re* necessity entails a synthetic necessary claim about the nature of reality. There are real, causal connections in the world, which causal connections Aquinas grounds in his concept of substantial form.

If the causal connection is not analytic, then it must be synthetic. Furthermore, since it is necessary, it cannot be *a posteriori*. Nelson argues, therefore, that this connection is synthetic *a priori* or synthetic necessary. It is a necessary connection, but one which is true of the world. Nelson suggests that his theory of causal necessities "…asserts that there is something that transcends what a phenomenalist, positivist, or strict empiricist would be willing to admit."[17] The realist overtones of Nelson's ontology are apparent; he adopts a form of ontological realism.

The absence of causal connections in a metaphysical system, Nelson argues, entails the following philosophical paradoxes:

> In fact, the assumption that there are only factual uniformities leaves us with a chaos: (a) *ontological* because everything would be completely independent of everything else; (b) *epistemological* because no inferential knowledge beyond the immediately given would be possible. [18]

Nelson concludes his analysis with the following remarks: "If the theory of the presuppositions of induction… is at least in principle sound, the only alternative to scepticism is the acknowledgment that some non-empirical metaphysics is true."[19] Commenting on the structure of Nelson's argument, Morris Weitz once wrote that each ontological category Nelson presented "… is presupposed as part of a network of ontological features without which our ordering of experience is incoherent…; they… are the very ontological features and structures which make knowledge possible." [20] This demonstrates that Nelson adopts both "ontological realism" and "epistemological realism."

Nomic universal propositions require the category of real causal connections, which are sortal properties. Furthermore, these causal relations, which are

---

18   *Ibid.*, p. 258 (italics not in the original).

19   *Ibid.*, p. 260.

20   Morris Weitz, "The Grounds of Sense," *Philosophy and Phenomenological Research*, Vol. 33, # 4 (June, 1973), p. 460. This is the best overall account of Nelson's ontological commitments found in the literature.

synthetic *a priori* connections in the world, are rooted in a substance. Nomic universal propositions presuppose an ontology of causal entities, which are the formal causal structures of the world. This is, in turn, what Aquinas meant by a *forma substantialis*. Nelson argues that a presupposition of mere uniformities alone is never sufficient to account for inductive knowledge. In his "A Defense of Substance," Nelson once wrote that the category of substance provides "... the connection presupposed by the *stable* compresence of qualities and... of dispositional properties (as well as) to connect the successive states of a series exemplifying a law."[21]

Weitz suggested that the theme running through Nelson's ontological studies was the search for what Weitz called "the grounds of sense."[22] In other words, how do philosophers go about making sense knowledge hang together in a consistent and thoughtful manner? For Nelson, the ultimate ontological category is substance. Like a primary substance in Aristotle and Aquinas, substance for Nelson is "...the ground of power, stability, order and causality in the world."[23] This is, it would appear, coextensive with an Aristotelian primary substance.

Therefore, what Nelson calls a synthetic necessary causal connection is similar structurally to what Aquinas means by a substantial form. A substantial form in Aquinas's metaphysics ties together the real connections in the world of sense. Without a substantial form, Aquinas could not argue for the difference between essential and accidental predications, or for a difference in properties upon which the predications are asserted. Nelson suggests that analytic philosophy, finely wrought, cannot sustain itself without metaphysical presuppositions. Aquinas would say the same about medieval Aristotelian philosophy. For Nelson, the two fundamental ontological categories are causality and substance. For Aquinas, the two categories are substantial form and primary substance. Weitz rendered the following summary statement on Nelson's ontology:

> Now since induction presupposes cause and cause presupposes substance, ... (Nelson's) solution for the validity of induction is a world that, whatever else it may have, contains synthetic causal connections among certain events that are unified in a substantive manner.[24]

Hence, if nomic universal propositions hold, it follows that reality must be structured by an ontological category of form. This analysis of induction put forward

---

21   *The Philosophical Review*, Vol. LVI, # 5 (September, 1947), p. 499. This is the printed version of Nelson's Pacific Division American Philosophical Association Presidential Address. Nelson was at that time a member of the faculty at the University of Washington before joining the faculty at The Ohio State University as Chair.

22   Weitz, *op cit.*

23   *Ibid.*, p. 466.

24   *Ibid.*

by Nelson offers one refutation to the Burnyeat thesis. This is, therefore, a dialectic that establishes the ontological necessity for the existence of natural kinds. This natural kind metaphysics is a necessary condition for ethical naturalism in Aquinas.[25]

## Thomas Aquinas and the *Summa Theologiae*

Given the recent renaissance of natural law, one needs to consider briefly the old questions of natural law and how these questions relate to the new look of contemporary philosophy rooted in a theory of natural kinds.[26] The classical canon of natural law theory is the set of relevant passages in Questions 90–97 from the *Prima Secundae* of the Aquinas's *Summa Theologiae*. In addition, a structurally similar account is found in Thomas's *Commentary on the Nicomachean Ethics*.

Two principal points need addressing in Aquinas's account of ethical naturalism rooted in the works of Aristotle: (a) the foundation of a theory of the human person and (b) the requirement of reason as opposed to voluntarism.

## The Human Person and the Requirements of Reason

Aquinas bases his moral theory, and *a fortiori* his theory of human or positive law and a derivative but not an explicit theory of human rights, on the foundation of the human person as an instance of a natural kind. Aquinas argues that a human person is, by definition, a substantial unity grounding a set of potentialities, capacities, or dispositions. The substantial form is the ontological ground for this set of dispositional properties. Aquinas divides these capacities into three generic headings, which serve as the basis of this theory of natural kinds for human persons. This is Aquinas's account of human nature – the human natural kind – which is based upon the insights of Aristotle's *Nicomachean Ethics*:[27]

---

25    A parallel way of approaching the need for form in contemporary philosophical discussions is in the area of philosophy of mind. This has been pursued by John Haldane. Taking his cues from philosophers who recently have defended some version of direct realism (Donald Davidson, John McDowell, Hilary Putnam, and Wilfred Sellars), Haldane has pointed to formal causality as the ontological basis of epistemology. See Haldane, "A Return to Form in the Philosophy of Mind," *op. cit.*, pp. 40–64, as well as "Insight, Inference and Intellection," in *Proceedings of the American Catholic Philosophical Association*, "Insight and Inference," Vol. 75, 1999 (Bronx, NY: Fordham University, 2000).

26    Those interested in this recent revival of natural law theory might consult the author's review essay on eight books in the *American Catholic Philosophical Quarterly*, forthcoming.

27    Thomas Aquinas, *Summa Theologiae*, I-II, Q. 94, a. 2.

1. The set of Living Dispositions (what humans share with plants);

2. The set of Sensitive Dispositions (what humans share with animals);

3. The set of Rational Dispositions (what renders humans unique in the material realm).

Thomas's ethical naturalism provides for the moral protection that prevents, in principle, the hindering of the development of the basic human dispositions. Considered schematically, a living disposition is the capacity or drive all living beings have to continue in existence. In human persons, this capacity is to be protected.[28] Had humans been created or evolved (e.g., evolution through the *rationes seminales* of Augustine) differently, a different set of proscriptions would hold. A protection is what it is because human nature is what it is. This analysis is similar structurally to what H. L. A. Hart in his discussion of the "natural necessities" in the *Concept of Law* called the human right to the protection against violence.[29]

In a similar fashion, one of the rational dispositions Aquinas considered is the drive human beings have to know – our innate curiosity to know and to understand. Aquinas suggests that this disposition is only developed when human persons know propositions that are true. Hence, human persons have a "moral claim" to the truth. Again, these basic claims protect what human persons are as human beings. Finnis once argued, for instance, that college faculty have an obligation not to teach that which is known to be false, because this fractures the right to true propositions, which right students as human persons possess intrinsically. Finnis offered the same principle for political, academic, and religious leaders. This is based upon the classic position of "a conception of human dignity and worth, precisely as it bears on the interpersonal act of communication."[30]

The English Dominican, Columba Ryan, once wrote that these three general aspects of human nature are "the good of the individual survival, biological good, and the good of human communication."[31] In his *The Morality of Law*,[32]

---

28  While both Finnis and Veatch, among others, have developed a theory of human rights from the writings of Aquinas, nonetheless there is not developed explicitly in Aquinas a theory of rights. The work of Brian Tierney might be consulted on these issues. However, a right is determined on the foundation of protecting the basic human dispositional properties.

29  H. L. A. Hart, *The Concept of Law* (Oxford: Oxford University Press, 1961), pp. 194 ff.

30  Finnis, *Aquinas: Moral, Political and Legal Theory* (Oxford: Oxford University Press, 1998), p. 160.

31  Columba Ryan, O.P., "The Traditional Concept of Natural Law: An Interpretation," in *Light on the Natural Law*, edited by Iltud Evans, O.P. (Baltimore: Helicon Press, Inc., 1965), p. 28.

Lon Fuller argued for communication as a necessary condition for what he referred to as substantive theory of natural law. Martin Golding referred to the living dispositions as the "basic requirements of human life," the sensitive dispositions as the "basic requirements for the furtherance of the human species," and the rational dispositions as "the basic requirements for the promotion of [a human person's] good as a rational and social being."[33] In his *Aquinas*, Finnis writes as follows:

> The order Aquinas has in mind is a metaphysical stratification: [1] what we have in common with all substances, [2] what, more specifically, we have in common with other animals, and [3] what is peculiar to us as human beings.[34]

Martha Nussbaum once suggested eight fundamental properties: "we can nonetheless identify (as) certain features of our common humanity, closely related to Aristotle's original list." Nussbaum's eight characteristics are mortality, the body, pleasure and pain, cognitive capability, practical reason, early infant development, affiliation or a sense of fellowship with other human beings, and humor.[35] In his *Natural Law and Natural Rights*, Finnis puts forward what he takes to be a list of basic human goods: life, knowledge, play, aesthetic experience, friendship, practical reasonableness, and religion.[36] The point here is that these theories of ethical naturalism depend upon the concept of the human person and require the "functioning well" of that person – all of which are rooted in Aristotle's concept of *eudaimonia* or "happiness." Furthermore, except for Finnis, *eudaimonia* is rooted in the natural kind of the human person, which is the metaphysical foundation necessary for moral theory in natural law theory. Moreover, the necessity of reason as opposed to will is emphasized continually in the writings of Thomas. Throughout his discussion of law-making and moral theory, Aquinas argues that reason is to be employed with vigor. Law is, as Aquinas emphatically states, "an ordinance of reason." A purely voluntarist account of either moral theory or jurisprudence, according to Aquinas, is incorrect.[37]

---

32   Lon Fuller, *The Morality of Law* (New Haven, CT: Yale University Press, 1964).

33   Martin Golding, "Aquinas and Some Contemporary Natural Law Theories," *Proceedings of the American Catholic Philosophical Association (1974)*, pp. 242–43.

34   Finnis, *Aquinas, op. cit.*, p. 81.

35   Nussbaum, "Non-Relative Virtues," in Martha Nussbaum and Amartya Sen (eds.), *The Quality of Life* (Oxford: Clarendon Press, 1993), pp. 263–64.

36   Finnis, *Natural Law and Natural Rights* (corr. ed.) (Oxford: Clarendon Press, 1982), pp. 85–92. Finnis argues that this set of basic goods is known by practical reason and not grounded in a philosophical anthropology. Haldane and this author have suggested that this awareness appears reducible to intuition as elucidated by Sir David Ross in *The Right and the Good*.

37   In contemporary jurisprudence, both Fuller and Golding defend versions of reason in opposition to voluntarism.

## The Naturalistic Fallacy and a Theory of Obligation

When considering natural law theory as a form of ethical naturalism, two important philosophical questions remain that need to be addressed:

1. The issue of the "naturalistic fallacy."

2. The derivation of a theory of obligation.

Briefly, a dispositional account of human essence enables Aquinas to transcend the naturalistic fallacy. The "good" is the end to be attained, which is the development of the dispositional property. Hence, a "value" is not added onto a fact; rather, a value is the further development of a dispositional fact. Disposition and end are in the same ontological category of natural properties, the former the formal cause and the latter the final cause. Neither Hume nor Moore considered the possibility of developmental or dispositional properties. In fact, the concept of a mathematical class dominates the discussion of essence in modern philosophy. Descartes dismissed the Aristotelian position on dispositional properties, and this dismissal has remained regnant through most modern and contemporary philosophical discussions of essence or class defining properties. Nothing is more opposed to a dispositional analysis than a mathematical concept of class.

Aquinas, next, adopts what might be called a "metaphysics of finality." Veatch uses this concept in several of his works, which is gleaned from the insights of R.-A. Gauthier, who first addressed the issues of the metaphysics of finality.[38] The ends to be attained are determined by the content of the natural kind of the human person; this differs radically from ordinary teleological theories like utilitarianism. Therefore, the dispositional view of human nature enables Aquinas's version of natural law theory not to succumb to the charges of the naturalistic fallacy and provides a justification for a theory of obligation. In other words, these ends ought to be obtained because of the very dispositional structure of human nature. The ends are not arbitrary because they are determined by the natural kind of human nature itself. Obligation is rooted in the ends themselves.

An important jurisprudential corollary follows from this analysis. The role that this theory of ethical naturalism contributes to successful law making should be apparent. Any law, which, all things being equal, hinders the development of a natural disposition in a human person, is inherently unjust. Aquinas provides a set of criteria by means of which a theory of natural rights could be developed, and from that, a justified theory of law. This jurisprudence derivation is, however, beyond the limits of this analysis. [39]

---

38  Veatch, *Swimming Against the Current in Contemporary Philosophy* (Washington, DC: Catholic University of America Press, 1990), p. 116; Veatch acknowledges his debt to Gauthier.

39  Aquinas argues that the common good – the commonweal – of a society must be

## Thin Versus Thick Theories of Human Nature

This natural law account based on a metaphysics of natural kinds suggests a moral and a jurisprudential limit for contemporary philosophers like Ronald Dworkin and John Rawls. Both adopt only a "thin theory" of the human good. Hence, their theories lack any substantive content based on the foundational principles of human nature, which is a theoretical problem with most theories of liberal jurisprudence. Liberalism in jurisprudence, by its very definition, denies any role for substantive content to the fabric of law making. Without the content that a theory of human person provides, jurisprudence is limited in its attempt at achieving a substantive theory of human rights. Rawls's person who has a passion for counting blades of grass in city squares or Dworkin's beer-drinking TV addict both may be leading a good life – one of "integral human fulfillment," to use a Finnis term – provided they have chosen these ends after mature reflection. A thick theory of human nature espoused by the ethical naturalism in the Aquinian scheme put forward in this essay requires more than what Rawls and Dworkin's thin theories permit. The same applies equally to the so called "good reasons moral philosophers" of the mid-twentieth century.

Robert George's *Making Men Moral*[40] addresses this set of issues with some dispatch, which contemporary philosophers refer to as "moral perfectionism." Moral perfectionism is consistent only within the context of a theory of the human person grounded on a theory of the natural kind of human nature. This natural law schema provides a set of properties that determine the content of the human good to be attained. Without this content, one falls quickly into the vacuum of formalism. Such formalism is, in many ways, the hallmark of Kantian moral theory, most "good reasons" moral theories, all legal positivism, much legal realism, and most liberal jurisprudence. One might ask what justifies a morally right action for Kant or a set of human rights for Dworkin or for Rawls? In the end, it is the exercise of reason itself – what contemporary moral philosophers often refer to as a "good reasons approach" to moral reasoning. What the natural law position offers, if only in a broad and general way, is a set of human properties or qualities – human nature – without which a justification

---

part of the enactment of a law. Finnis translates the common good as "the public good." A law is never justified for the private interest of one or a few citizens. Furthermore, the common good or the commonweal of a society must not be neglected arbitrarily through the enactment of a law. Like Aristotle before him, Aquinas believed that a human person, as a social person, achieved her development through the auspices of a society. Donne's claim that "No man is an island" would ring true to Aquinas. The recent work of Michael Sandel on the importance of community hearkens back to Aquinas on the common good; among other places, see Michael Sandel, "Morality and the Liberal Ideal," *The New Republic*, May 7, 1984, pp. 15–17.

40  Robert George, *Making Men Moral* (Oxford: Oxford University Press, 1993).

of a moral theory or a legal system – including a set of human rights – is sought in vain. Since human nature or essence depends upon the foundational structure of substantial form, the metaphysical issues addressed earlier are necessary conditions towards explicating a contemporary version of form and natural kind in analytic philosophy.

### Finite Human Nature and the Existence of God

The above analysis suggests that what Aquinas needs for a consistent account of natural law is a metaphysical theory of natural kinds. This is the first question Aquinas must answer in his ontology if he is to develop a theory of natural law. Once he has justified his theory of natural kinds, then his next ontological question arises: Is the individual instance of a natural kind itself self-explanatory and totally independent, or is it a dependent being? Aquinas regards this question of dependency as a second order metaphysical question.

However, what if a philosopher of natural kinds adopted an evolutionary theory holding something like this: "Well, natural kinds are what they are through some evolutionary process, and we really can't say anything more about them? They are just there!" At this particular juncture, Aquinas and his evolutionary colleague (EC) are on the same playing field. Both could, in principle, derive a theory of natural duties based on the developmental properties of human nature. EC believes that the development of a moral theory from his metaphysics is the best he can do.

What does Aquinas do here? Aquinas, to quote a favorite metaphor of Father Copleston,[41] must get EC on "the metaphysical chessboard." Aquinas must show EC that his analysis of human nature – even as a natural kind – entails that a human person is a dependent being. This requires the "essence/existence" distinction, an ontological distinction that EC, following Aristotle, is not keen about affirming.[42] Here Aquinas must convince EC that a dependent being – or "contingent being" in cosmological argument circles – demands a real relation with an independent, Necessary Being. God as the *"Actus Purus"* – existence itself – is what provides a response to the question about dependency. Here Aquinas would suggest that EC consider the *Tertia Via* in the *Prima Pars* of the *Summa Theologiae*, which is the argument that contingent beings entail a necessary being.

It is at this juncture in Aquinas's metaphysical scheme of natural kinds that God enters. God, as necessary being, provides the answer to this second order metaphysical question about the dependent character of individuals of natural

---

41  Cf. the Copleston/Russell BBC debate on the existence of God.

42  Cf. Joseph Owens, "Aristotle and Aquinas," in Norman Kretzmann and Eleonore Stump, *The Cambridge Companion to Aquinas* (Cambridge: Cambridge University Press, 1993), pp. 38–59.

kinds. However, one could construct a theory of natural law on the basis only of a natural kind ontology composed of dispositional properties. What Aquinas provides additionally is an explanation in terms of dependency. What EC has done with his moral theory, so Aquinas would suggest, is not to have developed a false moral theory but rather an incomplete metaphysical theory. On a related note, if one asks about an interpretation of scripture passages about human beings made in the image and likeness of God, Aquinas uses the exemplar language he adopted from Augustine and, *a fortiori*, from Plato. This is what Aquinas meant by eternal law.

Hence, Aquinas does have God and eternal law in his system. But this is the last set of questions to which he responds. He can develop a theory of ethical naturalism from his account of a human essence as a natural kind. It is only when one asks about ontological dependency, however, that God as a "Source of Existence" becomes significant philosophically. Given this account, one may question the validity of the Thomist theological/metaphysical approach discussed above as a necessary condition of Aquinas's theory of natural law. Aquinas can develop a consistent metaphysics of natural kinds without an appeal to a divine being. This alone can serve as the ontological ground for natural law in Aquinas.

## Conclusion

This concludes a somewhat rapid sojourn through the gardens of contemporary ontology and its connection with the necessary conditions for natural law theory. Natural kind theory in Aquinas is based upon the empirical principles he discovered in the Aristotelian texts, both those which came to Paris from the Islamic translating institute at Toledo and especially those texts that his Dominican confrere, William of Moerbeke, provided for him from the Middle East. This empiricism requires that "*Nihil est in intellectu quod non prius fuerit in sensu.*" This epistemological maxim asserts that human knowers become aware of the content – the concepts – of natural kinds through the empirical process worked out in Aristotle's *De Anima* and in Book Two of the *Posterior Analytics*, texts in the philosophy of mind in Aristotle that Aquinas appropriated almost *in toto*. Since moral theory is a second order activity for Aquinas, as it was for Aristotle, the concept of a human essence must be first determined. Aquinas nowhere suggests that one needs Divine knowledge to be aware of essences. Aquinas does not accept the theory of Divine Illumination proposed by Augustine.

This essay articulates a theoretical possibility for reconstructing the texts of Aquinas so that a version of natural law makes good philosophical sense without requiring as a necessary condition a position of Theological Definism. That Aquinas was a theologian and a philosopher no one denies. This essay, however, articulates the "logic" of his argument suggesting that the role of God in natural law theory is a final ontological question. Aquinas's hylomorphic metaphysics can account for the content of a human essence – the natural kind – without an appeal to the eternal law. There is no need, therefore, to appeal to a divine being in order to understand the content of a human essence. The foundation of natural law depends upon natural kinds, which is a metaphysical issue resolved in terms of Aquinas's metaphysics, not his theology.

The heritage of ethical naturalism, with its emphasis on natural law theory as found in Thomas Aquinas, has been re-discovered by contemporary analytic moral philosophers and philosophers of law. Several important issues formulated in the analytic tradition of moral and legal philosophy have their roots structurally aligned with the old questions posed by Thomas Aquinas in the central tradition of natural law theory. These issues in analytic philosophy pose a "new look" to some rather "old questions," but questions not relegated to the metaphysical pile of antiquated philosophical claims. This essay, then, provides "a new look at some old questions." The old questions reflect a tradition of moral realism that is important for normative ethical theory and for jurisprudence. Natural Law theory at its best has a realist foundation based on human persons actually living in the here and now of the twenty-first century. It is a theory with rationality articulated as a necessary condition. It is cognizant thoroughly of the common or public good. It is a theory well worth the attention of contemporary philosophers. Natural Law theory, once thought to be part of the dustbin of antiquated theories on the nature of law, is now providing vibrant excitement in writings found in contemporary moral theory and jurisprudence. Yet it demands a realist ontology of natural kinds. This essay has attempted to spell out how one might articulate that set of conditions by means of an analysis of the role of substantial form in contemporary metaphysical discussions. Hence, this essay is a "new look" at some "old questions"![43]

---

43   The author kindly acknowledges his friend, Fulvio Di Blasi, for the invitation to present the original version of this essay at the conference he organized at the University of Notre Dame in 2003; in addition, the author expresses his gratitude to another good friend, Josh Hochschild, for his thoughtful editorial suggestions in preparing this essay for publication. Earlier parts of this analysis were read at philosophy colloquia at the University of North Florida and at Kenyon College.

# Knowledge of the Good as Participation in God's Love

## Fulvio Di Blasi

Thomas Aquinas often suggests, not only that every creature naturally loves God above all things and more than itself, but also that our knowledge of the good essentially involves knowledge and love of God. Let us read, for example, the following passages:

> Because nothing is good except insofar as it is a likeness and participation of the highest good, the highest good itself is in some way desired in every particular good.[1]

> Every movement of a will whereby powers are applied to operation is reduced to God, as a first object of appetite (primum appetibile) and a first agent of willing (primum volentem).[2]

> To know that God exists in a general and confused way is implanted in us by nature, inasmuch as God is man's beatitude. For man naturally desires happiness, and what is naturally desired by man must be naturally known to him. This, however, is not to know absolutely that God exists; just as to know that someone is approaching is not the same as to know that Peter is approaching, even though it is Peter who is approaching; for many there are who imagine that man's perfect good which is happiness, consists in riches, and others in pleasures, and others in something else.[3]

---

1     Thomas Aquinas, *Commentary on Aristotle's Nicomachean Ethics*, trans. by C. I. Litzinger, O.P. (Notre Dame, Ind.: Dumb Ox Books, 1993), lect. 1, no. 11.

2     Thomas Aquinas, *Summa Contra Gentiles* (hereafter *CG*), III, ch. 67. Translations of the *Summa Contra Gentiles* are by Anton C. Pegis for book 1, by James F. Anderson for book 2, and by Vernon J. Bourke for book 3 (Notre Dame, IN: University of Notre Dame Press, 1975).

3     Thomas Aquinas, *Summa Theologiae* [hereafter *ST*], I, q. 2, a. 1 ad 1. Translations are by the Fathers of the English Dominican Province (New York: Benzinger, 1947). See also *CG*, I, 10–11; *ST*, I, q. 12; I-II, q. 3, a. 8.

Now, these are difficult words that do not seem to fit common morality, in which God does not seem to play such an important role. Broadly speaking, we face two possibilities: either Aquinas was so immersed in abstract metaphysical reflections that he lost sight of the most ordinary reality, or his metaphysics expresses in the most radical way the deepest meaning of ordinary ethical reality. I will defend the second thesis. And this is why I reported the third quotation, in which the idea emerges that for many *ordinary* people, to know and to love God can just mean to vaguely sense or realize that "someone is approaching."

In my opinion, the key to understanding Aquinas' view on this issue is the concept of *participation*, which I take in this paper as a purely philosophical concept. The best approach, accordingly, is to focus first on Aquinas' general thesis that every good of this world is good not "essentially" (*per suam essentiam*) but only by participation. This thesis entails that knowledge of created goods provides a mediate knowledge of God as the essential good. The second step is to focus on our act of knowledge of the good. The object of this act is the participated good and, through it, God as the essential good. At the same time, our knowledge of the good is itself a very special kind of participated good; its goodness consisting in a *formal* participation in God's *knowledge* of the good: that is, in His love of Himself and of creation in view of Himself. In other words, our act of knowledge of the good has both an objective aspect and a subjective aspect. Objectively, we know the good as participated – and thus as objectively revealing God as the essential good. Subjectively, we are able to know the participated good due to our formal participation in God's love. The third step is to focus on the idea of "someone approaching," an idea which alone would deserve more than an essay, but is here limited to only a short concluding remark.

Scholars are very familiar today with both a wide revival of the concept of practical knowledge[4] and an intense debate on the concept of ultimate end in both Aristotle and Aquinas.[5] I should say immediately that in the present paper

---

4    The widespread contemporary debate on practical knowledge is closely connected to the strong rediscovery of Aristotle's thought that was started in the second part of the last century by authors like Leo Strauss, Eric Voegelin, and Hannah Arendt. For a bibliographical survey of this phenomenon, see Franco Volpi, "The Rehabilitation of Practical Philosophy and Neo-Aristotelianism," in Robert C. Bartlett and Susan D. Collins (eds.), *Action and Contemplation* (New York: State University of New York Press, 1999), pp. 3–25. In the anglosaxon analytic world, the renewed attention to practical knowledge is related to the discussion of the "reasons for action" intended as a way to overcome the gaps created by the value-free approach to human action in moral, political, and legal philosophy. A pioneer work, in this direction, has certainly been done by Herbert Hart in his *The Concept of Law* (Oxford: Clarendon Press, 1961).

5    The Aristotelian debate on the ultimate end flared up after W. F. R. Hardie ["The Final Good in Aristotle's Ethics," *Philosophy* 40 (1965), pp. 277–95] suggested the

I do not want to focus on "practical knowledge" as such but on "knowledge of the good" generally speaking. The two concepts are often put together as if they were the same thing. This is a mistake. Practical knowledge, at least in Aquinas, is a secondary and specific instance of knowledge of the good that involves a means-end relationship in which the end, being actually wanted or desired, makes the means desirable (*dilectio electiva*) and becomes action. Knowledge of the good, simply speaking, is not practical but speculative.[6] Moreover, the current debate on the ultimate end appears too narrowly centered on the arguments from intentionality and from the natural desire given by Aquinas, especially in *ST*, I-II, q. 1, a. 4 (*Is there an Ultimate End for Human Life?*) and q. 3, a. 8 (*Does the Happiness of Man Consist in the Vision of the Divine Essence?*). The present paper does not focus on these arguments either. There are deeper metaphysical principles at the root of Aquinas' view on the ultimate end; these principles are, at the moment, my main concern.

In what follows, I will first offer a short introduction to the concepts of "good" and of "participation" (Section 1); these concepts will then be better elucidated further in the paper. In Section 2, I will address Aquinas' general thesis of the created good as participated. Then, in section 3, I will move toward the analysis of our act of knowledge of the good. Finally, in section 4, I will return briefly to the last passage quoted above on our necessary – but general and confused – knowledge of God.

## 1. Introducing the Concepts of "Good" and "Participation"

"Good" (*bonum*) is, for Aquinas, a transcendental concept because it signifies exactly the same reality as "being" (*ens*). Yet, the term "good" makes conceptually explicit something that in the use of "*ens*" remains implicit. This is why Aquinas says that "good" adds something to the *understanding* of "*ens*" (*super intellectum entis*): something that is not in the things (*in rerum natura*) but only in reason (*in ratione tantum*). Specifically, "good" adds to "*ens*" a conceptual

---

distinction between dominant end and inclusive end. It is worth noticing the critical approach to this issue offered by J. L. Ackrill, "Aristotle on *Eudaimonia*" [1974], in N. Sherman (ed.), *Aristotle's Ethics* (Lanham, Md.: Rowman & Littlefield, 1999), pp. 57–77. Among Thomists, the question is presently highly debated due to the claim that there are, not one but, many incommensurable ultimate ends of human life made by the so-called "new natural law theorists." The "new natural law theory" is strongly related to the "rehabilitation" of practical knowledge, and was initiated by a well known article written by Germain Grisez in 1965 ["The First Principle of Practical Reason: A Commentary on the Summa theologiae, 1–2, Question 94, Article 2," *Natural Law Forum*, 10 (1965)].

6    See, for example, *ST*, I-II, q. 3, a. 5, where Aquinas explains that "happiness (beatitude) consists in activity of the speculative intellect rather than the practical."

reference to the fact that the *esse* of the *ens*[7] is an act, which gives existence and *perfection* to the *ens*, and which is therefore what the *ens* itself tends toward. The concept of good, in other words, contains a conceptual reference to the actual – existing – *ens* being always an end and an object of an appetite: "*et inde est quod omnes recte diffinientes bonum ponunt in ratione eius aliquid quod pertinet ad habitudinem finis.*"[8]

This short but rather technical account reveals an important metaphysical view of reality. For Aquinas, the existing being is dynamic: i.e., it is an action and a completion at the same time. The existing being tends not only toward other things but also toward its own act; this is why it preserves itself and remains in existence instead of falling back into nothingness. Consequently, when we know the existing being we know it also as good: namely, as an end and the object of an appetite. Its being good, however, is nothing else than its *esse*; and to know the good is nothing else than to know the way in which things exist, or to know their *act(s)* – whether substantial or accidental. This is why Aquinas writes that "to be in act [...] constitutes the nature of the good (*esse igi-tur actu boni rationem constituit*)," or that "by nature, the good of each thing is its act and perfection (*naturaliter enim bonum uniuscuiusque est actus et per-fectio eius*)."[9] This is what we should keep in mind for the purposes of the present paper: that to look for "the nature of the good (*boni rationem*)" is to look for the "act" and "perfection" of things.

The concept of participation refers to a specific kind of causality: namely, the causality that is simultaneously required for the effect to exist. An example is my hand holding the book: in this case, when my hand ceases to act as a cause the book falls down. Another example is the light shining on the book: when the light ceases to act the book is not visible.[10] Whenever something is acting in a

---

7    I use the Latin "*ens*" and "*esse*" to avoid ambiguity, as in English they are both translated with "being."

8    For all the quotations in this paragraph see Thomas Aquinas, *De Veritate*, q. 21, a. 1.

9    *CG*, I, ch 37. See also, *De Veritate*, q. 21, a. 2 c.: "Existence itself, therefore, has the essential note of goodness. Just as it is impossible, then, for anything to be a being which does not have existence, so too it is necessary that every being be good by the very fact of its having existence (*Ipsum igitur esse habet rationem boni. Unde sicut impossibile est quod sit aliquid ens quod non habeat esse, necesse est ut omne ens sit bonum ex hoc ipso quod esse habet*)." Translations of the *Quaestiones Disputatae De Veritate* (hereafter *De Veritate*) are from St. Thomas Aquinas, *Truth* (Chicago: Henry Regnery Company, 1952) Volume I, questions i-ix, trans. Robert W. Mulligan, S.J., and Volume III, questions xxi-xxix, trans. Robert W. Schmidt, S.J.

10   See the famous passage in Aquinas on the "*per se*" series of efficient causes: "In efficient causes it is impossible to proceed to infinity 'per se' – thus, there cannot be an infinite number of causes that are 'per se' required for a certain effect; for instance, that a stone be moved by a stick, the stick by the hand, and so on to infin-

way that cannot be caused by its own nature, we must logically refer its action to an external cause able to cause it by essence, and we say that the relevant object *participates* in that cause. The suspended book participates in the power of my hand, and the visible book participates in the power of a luminous object. Participation, thus, is something real in things, and it means a simultaneous and external causal dependence of their actions or properties. This causal relation has two important characteristics: (1) that the action (whatever it is) of the participating object follows the actual direction given to it by the cause (the suspended book stays exactly where the hand holds it, and the visible book is visible according to the kind of light that is acting upon it); (2) that the action of the participating object makes it similar to the cause (the suspended book *as suspended* reveals something of the power of the hand, and the visible book *as visible* is similar to the light-source affecting it). This can be summarized by saying that, in participation, the effect *as effect* is similar to the cause *as cause* and obeys its teleology.

As soon as we focus on the fact that, for Aquinas, the very *esse* of things is participated, we can see why the concept of participation is so important in his metaphysics. For Aquinas, all things are actually dependent on God as their efficient, final, and exemplary cause – including rational agents' act of knowledge of the good, which act is an accidental perfection of their being. Hence, the thesis that our act of knowledge of the good is participated entails: [1] that God simultaneously causes it as knowledge of the good (participation in God as efficient cause); [2] that our act involves love of the same ultimate end that God loves in causing it (participation in God as final cause); and [3] that our knowledge of the good is similar to God's own knowledge of the good (participation in God as exemplary cause).[11]

## 2. Created Good as Participated

In *De Veritate*, q. 21, a. 5, Aquinas, following "*Augustinum, Boetium et*

---

ity. But it is not impossible to proceed to infinity 'accidentally' as regards efficient causes; for instance, if all the causes thus infinitely multiplied should have the order of only one cause, their multiplication being accidental, as an artificer acts by means of many hammers accidentally, because one after the other may be broken. It is accidental, therefore, that one particular hammer acts after the action of another; and likewise it is accidental to this particular man as generator to be generated by another man; for he generates as a man, and not as the son of another man. For all men generating hold one grade in efficient causes – viz. the grade of a particular generator. Hence it is not impossible for a man to be generated by man to infinity; but such a thing would be impossible if the generation of this man depended upon this man, and on an elementary body, and on the sun, and so on to infinity" (*ST*, I, q. 46, a. 2 ad 7).

11 See, *ST*, I, q. 6, a. 4: "each thing is called 'good' by the divine goodness, as by the first exemplar, efficient, and final principle of goodness in its entirety."

*auctorem libri De Causis*," explains that the created good is said to be participated in a threefold way: as to the accidental good; as to the essential or substantial good; and as to the order to the first cause (*secundum ordinem ad causam primam*). Aquinas puts the accidental good first because, for him, something is said to be good absolutely speaking due, not to its substantial being, but to its accidental being. For my purposes, however, it is better to follow an ontological order and start with the essential or substantial good.

### 2.1. Substantial Good as Participated

The essential good of something is the act, or *esse*, that makes it existent according to its nature (man, tree, etc.). The essential principles of each *ens*, explains Aquinas, are what make it perfect in order for it to exist – "*In se ipso autem aliquid perficitur ut subsistat per essentialia principia*." As I just mentioned, Aquinas adds that, as far as these principles are concerned, something is good only *secundum quid* because a creature, in order to be good absolutely speaking, must be good (or *in act*) according to both the essential and the accidental principles. (An existing human being, for example, is certainly good according to the act of existence of his nature but can still be either morally good or morally evil. When we say, "This is a good man!," we refer, simply speaking, to his moral personality.) This is not my focus, though. My focus is on participation. Why is the creature's essential good participated? The answer to this question is that, except in the case of God, the essence of things does not logically include their existence; otherwise their natures could give existence to themselves and they would never die or be corrupted. It is logically possible to think of a man as not existent. Thus, when a man exists, it means that he has *esse* only by participating in what possesses *esse* by essence; and this can only be God.[12] The *esse* of limited beings is like the visibility of the book; if God ceases to create the book *disappears*. The *esse* of limited beings, as the result of God's creative action, is both similar to God's *esse* and ordered to the end for the sake of which God creates.

### 2.2. Accidental Good as Participated

More difficult appears the question of the accidental good, because accidents by definition exist, not in themselves, but in the substance's act. In point of fact, to say that the accidents' good participates in the substance's good – which is in turn participated – does not look very interesting; and Aquinas' discussion in *De Veritate*, q. 21, a. 5 seems to be no more than an homage paid to a statement made by Augustine. However, the same thesis is strongly restated in *ST*, I, q. 6, a. 3; and without any explicit reference to Augustine. This fact calls for more

---

12  See, *ST*, I, q. 44, a. 1.

attention to the relevant text in *De Veritate*, q. 21, a. 5; particularly where Aquinas writes, "Now it is by its essential principles that a thing is fully constituted (*perficitur*) in itself so that it subsists; but it is not so perfectly constituted as to stand as it should in relation to everything outside itself (*ut debito modo se habeat ad omnia quae sunt extra ipsium*) except by means of accidents added to the essence, because the operations by which one thing is in some sense joined to another proceed from the essence through powers distinct from it. Consequently nothing achieves goodness absolutely unless it is complete in both its essential and its accidental principles."

Aquinas sees the accidents as the metaphysical principles that relate the *ens* to the other things external to it (*ad omnia quae sunt extra ipsum*). Movement, for example, is always an interaction. But we might also think of color as the relation between the visible objects and the sense of sight; or of mass as the attractive relation of material bodies with each other; or even of our intelligence as the relation of our mind with every other reality (including ourselves as reflexively known to us). Now, a principle connecting the *existence* of two or more things with each other – i.e., making them *co-exist* in the same universe – cannot come from one of them unless this one is the creator of the other(s). So, the fact that limited things interact with each other due to their accidents calls for a transcendent cause in which they participate *as interacting with each other*: that is to say, according to their accidents. If I understand Aquinas correctly on this point, the metaphysical principle grounding his idea of the accidental good as participated coincides with his key idea that there is an *order* in nature: namely, that things act naturally in a way that is at the same time intelligible and harmonious. Aquinas always explains this point by referring to the notions of 'part' and 'whole.' His point is very refined because to say that there is an order means exactly to say that there is a whole in which things make sense as parts. And this, in turn, means, not only that the good of the whole as such is the ultimate meaning of the good of the parts as parts, but also that every part must be inclined to the good of the whole before and more than it is inclined to its own good as part. After all, this is the reason for the existence of the specific movement of each *part*: to contribute to the existence of the whole. If this were not so, the order itself (the whole) could not exist.

Whatever we might think of this argument, Aquinas takes it very seriously. This is why he states that all creatures, including men and angels, love God before themselves and with a greater love. "Not only man, so long as his nature remains unimpaired (*in suae integritate naturae*), loves God above all things and more than himself, but also every single creature, each in its own way, i.e. either by an intellectual, or by a rational, or by an animal, or at least by a natural love, as stones do, for instance, and other things bereft of knowledge, because each part naturally loves the common good of the whole more than its own particular good. This is evidenced by its operation, since the principal inclination of each part is toward common action conducive to the good of the whole. It may also be seen in civic virtues whereby sometimes the citizens suffer damage even to their own property and persons for the sake of the common good."[13] In *ST*, I, q. 60, a. 5, more or less with the same words, the same principle is specifically applied to the natural inclination, or natural love, of the will of both men and angels: "Consequently, since God is the universal good, and under this good both man and angel and all creatures are comprised, because every creature in regard to its entire being naturally belongs to God, it follows that from natural love angel and man alike love God before themselves and with a greater love."[14] It might be helpful to recall that the existence of a natural order is also the starting point of the fifth way to prove the existence of God – which, in turn, coincides with the philosophical proofs given by Aquinas for the existence of providence and of the eternal law.[15]

---

13   *ST*, II-II, q. 26, a. 3 c.

14   This is the whole relevant passage: "Now, in natural things, everything which, as such, naturally belongs to another, is principally, and more strongly inclined to that other to which it belongs, than toward itself. Such a natural tendency is evidenced from things which are moved according to nature: because 'according as a thing is moved naturally, it has an inborn aptitude to be thus moved,' as stated in *Phys.* ii, text. 78. For we observe that the part naturally exposes itself in order to safeguard the whole; as, for instance, the hand is without deliberation exposed to the blow for the whole body's safety. And since reason copies nature, we find the same inclination among the social virtues; for it behooves the virtuous citizen to expose himself to the danger of death for the public weal of the state; and if man were a natural part of the city, then such inclination would be natural to him. Consequently, since God is the universal good, and under this good both man and angel and all creatures are comprised, because every creature in regard to its entire being naturally belongs to God, it follows that from natural love angel and man alike love God before themselves and with a greater love (*naturali dilectione etiam Angelus et homo plus et principalius diligat Deum quam seipsum*). Otherwise, if either of them loved self more than God, it would follow that natural love would be perverse, and that it would not be perfected but destroyed by charity."

15   See, e.g., *CG*, III, ch. 64: "Moreover, that natural bodies are moved and made to operate for an end, even though they do not know their end, was proved by the fact that what happens to them is always, or often, for the best; and, if their workings resulted from art, they would not be done differently. But it is impossible for things that do not know their end to work for that end, and to reach that end in an orderly way, unless they are moved by someone possessing knowledge of the end, as in the case of the arrow directed to the target by the archer. So, the whole working of nature must be ordered by some sort of knowledge. And this, in fact, must lead back to God, either mediately or immediately, since every lower art and type of knowledge must get its principles from a higher one, as we also see in the speculative and operative sciences. Therefore, God governs the world by His providence. Furthermore, things that are different in their natures do not come together into one order unless they are gathered into a unit by one ordering agent. But in the whole of reality things are distinct and possessed of contrary natures; yet all come together in

## 2.3. *"Secundum Ordinem ad Causam Primam"*

"A still further difference is discovered between the divine goodness and that of
creatures. Goodness has the character of a final cause. But God has this, since
He is the ultimate end of all beings just as He is their first principle. From this
it follows that any other end has the status or character of an end only in relation to the first cause (*secundum ordinem ad causam primam*), because a secondary cause does not influence the effect unless the influence of the first cause
is presupposed, as is made clear in *The Causes*. Hence too, good, having the
character of an end, cannot be said of a creature unless we presuppose the relation of Creator to creature (*ordine creatoris ad creaturam*)."[16] The key words
here are, "because a secondary cause does not influence the effect unless the
influence of the first cause is presupposed." This principle is more explicit in
*CG*, book 3, ch. 17, "Now, the supreme agent does the actions of all inferior
agents by moving them all to their actions and, consequently, to their ends.
Hence, it follows that all the ends of secondary agents are ordered by the first
agent to His own proper end. Of course, the first agent of all things is God [...]
There is no other end for His will than His goodness, which is Himself [...]
Therefore, all things [...] are ordered to God as to their end."

In order to understand Aquinas on this point we must remember that the
concept of good involves the appetite for an end. Now, except in the case of God
– in Whom there is no real distinction between His appetite and His being –
appetite implies *movement*; and every movement, in Aristotle and Aquinas'
metaphysics, requires participation in a first Unmoved Mover. It goes without
saying that when God moves something, He cannot but do it according to His
end, which is Himself. And it goes without saying that at stake here are not the
extrinsic movements of things, but the intrinsic movements of their beings: that
is to say, their *natural inclinations*.[17] This same argument is specifically applied
by Aquinas also to the human will, which under this respect is not different from
any other participated appetite – for "to give natural inclinations is the sole prerogative of Him Who has established the nature. So also, to incline the will to
anything is the sole prerogative of Him Who is the cause of the intellectual

---

    one order, and while some things make use of the actions of others, some are helped
    or commanded by others. Therefore, there must be one orderer and governor of the
    whole of things."

16   *De Veritate*, q. 21, a. 5 c.

17   See *De Veritate*, q. 22, a. 1 c.: "What is directed or inclined to something by anoth-
    er is inclined to that which is intended by the one inclining or directing it. The arrow,
    for example, is directed to the same target at which the archer aims. Consequently,
    since all natural things have been inclined by a certain natural inclination toward
    their ends by the prime mover, God, that to which everything is naturally inclined
    must be what is willed or intended by God."

nature."[18] Therefore, if it is true that our moving world requires an Unmoved Mover, it necessarily follows that every nature – or natural inclination – and every appetite depends on God as "a first agent of willing (*primum volentem*)" (efficient cause) and tend to God "as a first object of appetite (*primum appetibile*) (final cause)."[19]

### 3. Our Knowledge of the Good as Participated

Let us shift our focus now to our act of knowledge of the good. On the basis of what was explained above, we should already be able to conclude that, as an accidental perfection of our being, this act is a participation in the order God gave to creation. As such, it tends chiefly to God as to the end of the whole of creation: that is to say, through this act we love God before ourselves and with a greater love. Moreover, as our knowledge of the good involves the movement of an appetite, it requires the creative action of God as Unmoved Mover. Thus, it participates in God as "a first agent of willing" and tends to God "as a first object of appetite."

So far so good. However, as correct as these conclusions might be theoretically, they do not look very satisfactory when what is at stake is an act as complex as our act of knowledge of the good. Unquestionably, we need a more specific approach to the nature of this act and to the supposed need for it to be participated. And, first of all, we need to focus on what exactly "knowledge of the good" means compared with the concept of good in general.

### 3.1. "Good" and "Knowledge of the Good"

"Good," as we recalled above, means that the *ens* is always an end and an object

---

18   *CG*, III, ch. 88.

19   *CG*, III, ch. 67. Here it might be helpful to recall also *CG*, II, ch. 23, in which Aquinas argues that the first unmoved mover must be a voluntary agent. This theses complements the first way by qualifying the unmoved mover as a rational agent. Let us read, for example, the following passages from chapter 23: "that which acts by itself is prior to that which acts by another (*quod per se agit, prius est eo quod per aliud agit*), for whatever is by another [*per aliud*] must be referred to that which is by itself (*per se*); otherwise, we fall into an infinite regress. A thing that is not master of its own action, however, does not act by itself; it acts as directed by something else (*ab alio actus*), not as directing itself (*seipsum agens*). Hence, the first agent mast act as master of His own action. But it is only by will that one is master of his own action. It follows, therefore, that God, who is the first agent, acts by His will (*per voluntatem agere*), not by necessity of His nature (*non per naturae necessitatem*)"; "To the first agent belongs the first action, even as the first motion pertains to the first thing movable. But the will's action is naturally prior to that of nature. For that which is more perfect is prior in nature, though in one and the same particular thing it be temporally posterior."

of an appetite – without appetite for an end, properly speaking, there is no good. "Knowledge," on the other hand, means, for both Aristotle and Aquinas, "intentional possession of a form." "Knowledge of the good," accordingly – whether sentient or intellectual – , must mean "intentional possession of the form of something *as* object of an appetite." But, in turn, being "knowledge of the good" an act – and therefore a good – of the knower, it cannot but happen *by way of appetite.* "Knowledge of the good," therefore, means to tend toward the *ens* by means of a form [of something *as* object of an appetite] intentionally possessed by the agent. In the knowledge of the good, the possessed form and the inclination of the appetite coincide.[20]

In the case of rational beings, "knowledge of the good" means at the same time: (a) to have an intellectual knowledge of the *ens* as object of an appetite; and (b) to tend toward it as intellectually known, or to love it by way of what we call 'rational appetite.' The intellectual knowledge of the good is nothing else than a sort of *inclined knowledge*: that is, an appetite for the *ens* understood as an end. This is why Aquinas seems to suggest that to know the good and to will the good are the same thing: "For, since the understood good (*bonum intellectum*) is the proper object of the will, the understood good is, as such, willed. Now, that which is understood is by reference to one who understands (*intellectum autem dicitur ad intelligentem*). Hence, he who grasps the good by his intellect (*intelligens bonum*) is, as such, endowed with will (*volens*)."[21]

For my purposes, it is important to notice that it is our very act of (intellectual) knowledge of the good – this accidental perfection of our being – that needs to be participated. As the luminous object participates *as luminous* in what possesses the light by essence, and as every created good participates *as appetite for ens* in what is essentially good, so our intellectual knowledge of the good should formally participate *as intellectual knowledge of the good* – that is, as a (rational) appetite for the *ens* known as an end – in God's knowledge as the cause of every good. This means, in turn, that our participation must formally happen – at the intellectual level – by way of *inclination* to God *known* as the "first agent of willing" and as the ultimate end (*primum appetibile*) of both ourselves and the whole universe; and also as the exemplary cause of everything.

---

20   This does not mean that the "known good" is necessarily "practical," but only that it cannot be known *as good* without the inclination of the appetite. This is why animals know as good only the things toward which their sentient appetite tend; whereas we know as good every *ens* insofar as it fits the inclination to the (intelligible) truth that we call will. To *know* a beautiful panorama means to *love* it, even if there is nothing we can do with it (i.e., even if it is not a practical object of our knowledge). God *loves* even non-created worlds because He knows them as something He does not want to create: that is to say, He loves these worlds insofar as they are known to Him, but He does not love them according to His practical knowledge.

21   CG, I, ch. 72.

But, does Aquinas offer any specific argument in support of these things? The answer is "Yes, the doctrine of the active intellect!"

### 3.2. The Need for the Active Intellect

For both Aristotle and Aquinas, knowledge, whether sentient or intellectual, is an actualization of a receiver (or passive) knowing faculty caused by the act of the known object as knowable. For instance, the visible object as visible (in act) causes the act of seeing it in the visual faculty. There are two important principles at stake here: one is that the object known must be in act in order to be known; and the other is that to know is an act of the knowing faculty. We can think of a file (known object) saved on a floppy disk (knowing faculty). What we call "file" should exist (be in act) before – and while – being saved; and the saved file is no more than the floppy disk configured (actualized) in a particular way. Now, the reason we need the active intellect to know the truth (whether theoretical or practical) is that *the universals* that our (passive) intellect receives when it knows things through the senses do not exist as such – as universals – in the (particular) things known. In other words, the intelligible objects do not exist as intelligible except in the intellect that knows them; thus, our intellect must be able to abstract them (i.e., to turn them from potentiality into actuality) before receiving them – as if the floppy-disk had to make the file a file before receiving it into itself as a file. The key point is that our intellect, in order to make the intelligible species an intelligible species, must be already in act as intellect *before* possessing any actual knowledge at all. I say "as intellect" because this first act of the intellect as a knower must be *similar* to the known object as known: that is, as intelligible. Knowledge is always a question of similarity. Strictly speaking, we can say that the passive intellect does not *exist* without any knowledge making it actual, but that the active intellect is *subsistent*.

This point should be clearer if we focus more on the relevant difference between sense knowledge and intellectual knowledge. In the case of sense knowledge, the knowing faculty is actualized by the act of the material thing as perceptible.[22] In the case of intellectual knowledge, there is no act of the material thing as intelligible. If the material individual thing were in act intelligible it would not be individual and it would not be material. Therefore, unlike sense knowledge, in the case of intellectual knowledge the act of the intelligible object is caused by the knowing faculty itself. The intellect, in other words, *moves* itself

---

22   As is well known, for both Aristotle and Aquinas, the act of the sentient faculty and the act of the thing perceived are one and the same act. See, Aristotle, *On the Soul*, III, 425b26–426a27; Aquinas, *in de Anima*, III, 2, 425b22–426a26 [*Commentary on Aristotle's De Anima*, trans. K. Foster, O.P. and S. Humphries, O.P. (Notre Dame, IN: Dumb Ox Books, 1994), pp. 184–85, nn. 592–96].

by causing the act of the intelligible object as intelligible in order to receive it as an intelligible species.[23]

### 3.3. The Participation of the Active Intellect

The reason why our active intellect requires God's causality is that it is a *moved mover* of what is intelligible. The active intellect causes the acts of the intelligible objects as intelligible but does not create their intelligibility. This is why our intellect is still a *receiver* of knowledge and does not know everything already; rather, "it reaches to the understanding of truth by arguing, with a certain amount of reasoning and movement. Again it has an imperfect understanding; both because it does not understand everything and because, in those things which it does understand, it passes from potentiality to act" – Human intellect is "mobile" and "imperfect."[24] As a *moved mover* of what is intelligible, which knows according to *degrees of knowledge*, the active intellect fits the rationale of both the first and the fourth ways to prove the existence of God given in *ST*, I, q. 2, a. 3. That is to say, the existence of the active intellect requires: (1) the existence of a first intellect that moves every act of understanding without being moved; and (2) the existence of an intellect that possesses what is intelligible at the highest degree, and in which every lower degree of intellectual knowledge participates. This train of reasoning is clear in *ST*, I, q. 79, a. 4; and it is ultimately the reason that Aquinas thinks the active intellect receives its "intellectual light" (its first act) directly from God's intellect – the active intellect makes us able partially to see things as they are in God's mind.[25]

For Aquinas, "*ens*" is the first notion of intellectual knowledge, and "*ens in universali*," or "*ens universale*" (universal being), is the common object of this knowledge.[26] The concept of "*ens*" and the concept of "intelligibility" go together. To know something intellectually and to know it *as ens* (being) are the same thing; everything is intelligible insofar as it *is* (a table, a dog, red, tall,

---

23  "Since [...] forms existing in matter are not actually intelligible; it follows that the natures of forms of the sensible things which we understand are not actually intelligible. Now nothing is reduced from potentiality to act except by something in act; as the senses are made actual by what is actually sensible. We must therefore assign on the part of the intellect some power to make things actually intelligible, by abstraction of the species from material conditions. And such is the necessity for an active intellect" (*ST*, I, q. 79, a. 3 c).

24  *ST*, I, q. 79, a. 4 c.

25  On the participation of the active intellect in God's intellect, besides *ST*, I, q. 79, a. 4, see also q. 84, a. 5, where Aquinas specifies that we receive from God the "intellectual light" but not "the intelligible species, which are derived from things."

26  See *De Veritate*, q. 1, a. 1; and *ST*, I, q. 78, a. 1.

pleasant, Sicilian, etc.). The analogical notion of *ens* – analogical because no specific difference can add something to it as if this something were not *ens* – precedes, therefore, every particular intellectual knowledge and constitutes, so to speak, the glasses through which we see reality *as intelligible*. Hence, to say that our intellect tends to know the truth is equivalent to say that our intellect tends to know the *ens* as *ens* (i.e., the *is* of *being*).

As we saw already, our knowledge of each particular *ens* reveals a real distinction between its *being* (*esse*) and its being *something* (*essence*) – "this is a pencil," but "is" is not only of the pencil. We have already focused on the need for the creatures' *esse* to participate in an efficient and final cause that *is* by essence. Now we should focus on the need for the creature's *esse* to be an imitation of this cause.

*Esse* is common to everything and indeterminate: i.e., it can exist according to every possible essence. Essence, on the other hand, in a sense limits the being to a specific way of being. Every particular knowledge of the *ens* reveals, therefore, a *limitation* of the infinite possibilities of *esse*; but it reveals also a real *imitation* of what possesses *esse by essence*. This corresponds exactly, from the side of our knowledge, to the way in which, for Aquinas, God knows everything through the knowledge of Himself: "the divine essence comprehends within itself the nobilities of all beings [...] according to the mode of perfection. Now, every form, both proper and common [...] is a certain perfection [...] The intellect of God therefore, can comprehend in His essence that which is proper to each thing by understanding wherein the divine essence is being imitated and wherein each thing falls short of its perfection. Thus, by understanding His essence as imitable in the mode of life and not of knowledge, God has the proper form of a plant; and if He knows His essence as imitable in the mode of [sense] knowledge and not of intellect, God has the proper form of animal, and so forth. Thus, it is clear that, being absolutely perfect, the divine essence can be taken as the proper exemplar of singulars. Through it, therefore, God can have a proper knowledge of all things."[27]

In short: our knowledge of (limited) *entia* reveals their being causally dependent on what has *esse* as its own essence. On the one hand, the existence is not logically required by the essence of what is not its own *esse* – the actual existence of limited beings (their *esse*) requires a creative action by what exists by essence. On the other hand, the plurality and gradation of the (common) *esse* in the existing things requires a single subsistent, exemplar, cause that has the *esse* at the highest degree.[28] This is how Aquinas proves the necessity of creation: "all beings apart from God are not their own being, but are beings by

27    *CG*, I, ch. 54.
28    On this type of causality see also Aquinas, *Quaestio disputata De Potentia*, q. 3, a. 5.

participation. Therefore it must be that all things which are diversified by the diverse participation of being, so as to be more or less perfect, are caused by one First Being, Who possesses being most perfectly."[29]

Our intellectual knowledge is always in tension between the *immediate* knowledge of limited ways of being and the *mediate* knowledge of the Being that has in itself the fullness of being, and that is at the same time (a) the efficient cause, (b) the exemplary cause, and (c) the final cause of them. Intellectual curiosity is our tendency to go always beyond a specific essence toward a fuller understanding of universal being: our constantly fleeing the (limiting) essence.[30] If this is true, Aquinas should have defined intellectual knowledge with reference to God as its ultimate object: namely, as the final cause of the knowledge of truth, or as the end toward which the knowledge of truth ultimately tends.

In point of fact, this is exactly what he did. He did it in the treatise on law at the exact moment of indicating the inclination specifically distinguishing man from lower natures, "Thirdly, there is in man an inclination to good, according to the nature of his reason, which nature is proper to him: thus man has a natural inclination to know the truth about God, and to live in society."[31] At first glance, this passage might appear strangely reductive with respect to our inclination to know the truth. However, it is fairly accurate as it refers our inclination to the truth to its ultimate object and to our openness to the *ens in universali*.

### 3.4. Ens Universale and Bonum Universale

"For the will must be commensurate with its object. But the object of the will is a good grasped by the intellect (*bonum intellectum*), as stated above. Therefore, it is of the nature of will to reach out to whatever the intellect can propose to it under the aspect of goodness (*sub ratione boni*)."[32] If our intellect knows everything in the light of universal being, and so reaches the knowledge of a first efficient, final and exemplary cause, Aquinas can legitimately attribute the same scope to our rational appetite. Thus, to the *ens universale* corresponds, on the will's side, the *bonum universale*, which determines the nature and ultimate end of our desire. The passage we quoted at the beginning – "Because nothing is good except insofar as it is a likeness and participation of the highest good, the highest good itself is in some way desired in every particular good" – should

---

29   *ST*, I, q. 44, a. 1 c.
30   See, on this tension in our knowledge, Cornelio Fabro, *Dall'essere all'esistente* (Brescia: Morcelliana, 1965), pp. 60–69.
31   *ST*, I-II, q. 94, a. 2 c. On the reason why this inclination refers only to the intellect and not to the will, see Lawrence Dewan, "St. Thomas, John Finnis, and the Political Good," *The Thomist* 64 (2000), 337–74.
32   *CG*, II, ch. 27.

now make more sense: since we know the goods of this earth in the light of the universal good, it is impossible for us to know them without, at the same time, knowing and desiring through them their first cause, "the highest good itself."

### 4. "Someone is Approaching"

It is time now to go back to the last passage quoted at the beginning:

> To know that God exists in a general and confused way is implanted in us by nature, inasmuch as God is man's beatitude. For man naturally desires happiness, and what is naturally desired by man must be naturally known to him. This, however, is not to know absolutely that God exists; just as to know that someone is approaching is not the same as to know that Peter is approaching, even though it is Peter who is approaching; for many there are who imagine that man's perfect good which is happiness, consists in riches, and others in pleasures, and others in something else.

It is important to go back to what this passage means because otherwise Aquinas' ethical foundation would be, maybe consistent, but a bit odd. It is obvious that not many people think of God when they act morally; and everybody has experience of good people who even do not believe in God. What does it mean, therefore, that the very knowledge of the good is knowledge and love of God? As we can see in the passage above, what Aquinas means is much more nuanced than it might appear at a first and superficial glance. What we necessarily need when we know the good is to see that "Someone [the highest good] is approaching." This is a necessary (mediate) knowledge that can be "general and confused," and that does not mean "to know God absolutely speaking." It does mean, however, that knowledge of the good has an absolute and transcendental character. This thesis corresponds to what Aquinas says in *ST*, I-II, q. 5, a. 8; namely, that "every man necessarily desires happiness" "according to the general notion of happiness" (*secundum communem rationem beatitudinis*); but with regard to the content of the ultimate end (*secundum specialem rationem quantum ad id in quo beatitudo consistit*), "not all desire happiness." For Aquinas, in order to know and to love God "absolutely" we cannot do without "reasoning" and without morally good behavior.

Now, the idea that we know the good only when we know that "the highest good is approaching" is not only extremely interesting, but also very beautiful. After all, what does it mean to act morally – i.e., according to conscience – if not to act on the assumption that what is good transcends both you and me, and so ought to be done? From this viewpoint, the person who tries sincerely to act morally without believing in God, even without realizing it, is on his or her way toward knowing God "absolutely." Whereas the immoral person damages and distorts his or her own intellectual nature by eclipsing the vision of the "highest good" that is approaching with the selfishness of his or her concupiscence; or, in a sense, by putting or forcing down the transcendental character of the good.

Let me conclude by saying that there are many features of moral experience that reveal its transcendental character. After all, moral experience is the paradox of fulfilling oneself by forgetting or sacrificing oneself. It is the desire for *absolute* moral truths, and of an absolute happiness and justice that are not possible in this world. Many people make strong moral decisions only when they get to thinking of God. The so-called "good atheist" ought eventually to find his way to God. Otherwise he cannot be entirely good, he will embrace some kind of idolatry, and he will finally frustrate his nature and the natures of people around him.

# The Role of God in Aquinas's Ethical Thought: Can an Atheist Be Moral?

## Giacomo Samek Lodovici

In this paper I will consider the role of God in Aquinas's ethical thought. Leaving aside the question of the theological basis of ethics, I want to focus on the question of the role of theological belief in ethical action. In other words I will try to give an answer to this question: "can an atheist be moral?"

### The formulation of Thomistic ethics

In order to understand the importance of God in Aquinas's ethical thought we must examine the object of his *moralis consideratio*.

I will begin with Nietzsche's very incisive objection to ethics as a whole. It is an objection that attacks moral life as a paradigm of frustration and sacrifice, of constraints and duties, of restrictions and negations imposed on man – as a system of binding rules which stifles our spontaneity and oppresses our freedom. The moral praxis, according to this objection, produces a frustrating life characterized by misery, manifesting a contempt towards the present life, a life which is subordinated to a vain promise of future, eschatological happiness.

Now, this objection reveals a weakness in secular formulations of morality. As S. Pinckaers[1] underlines, moral thought has been deeply transformed through history. Its basic formulation has shifted from the concepts of self-fulfilment, happiness and virtue, to the notions of obligation, rule, law and duty. The first formulation is typical of the classical tradition through Aquinas;[2] the second is instead typical of almost all modern moral reflection.

Given this development, the first problems and the most important questions which ethics today must answer are: What are the rules of right behavior?

---

1     S. Pinckaers, *Les sources de la morale chrétienne. Sa méthode, son contenu, son histoire* (Fribourg : Editions Universitaires Fribourg Suisse, 1985), chapter 1.

2     But F. Di Blasi, *Dio e la legge naturale. Una rilettura di Tommaso d'Aquino* (Pisa: ETS, 1999), English version *God and the Natural Law: A Rereading of Aquinas* (South Bend, IN: St. Augustine's Press, 2001), differently from Pinckaers, explains that Suarez still assigns a consistent role to the ultimate end in his ethics.

What must we do? What is allowed? What is forbidden? What prohibitions must we never transgress? The notion of duty becomes so controlling that moral inquiry will concern only those human acts which are subordinated to a duty. In this way, ethics becomes the science of duties and obligations. It is clear that this modern emphasis ignores man's *end*, and moral life is easily marked by frustration, as Nietzsche says.

On the contrary, in classical ethics the main questions which all ethical reflection must confront are: How can I carry out a good or worthy life? What is the best way of living?[3] How can I obtain self-fulfilment? Thomistic moral science is the science of human acts, both in general (*Summa Theologiae* I-II) and in particular (*ST* II-II); the totality of human acts forms the *motus rationalis creaturae in Deum*, and sets up the framework of Thomistic ethics of the *Secunda Pars*.[4] But the *motus rationalis creaturae in Deum* coincides with the dynamism and the overall movement of man towards *self-fulfilment* and *happiness*, which are the very keystone of moral philosophy; as the last aim, they give moral reflection its general orientation. The whole structure of *Secunda Pars* directly depends on the answer to the question of self-fulfilment.

## The fundamental inclinations

In light of the above, I can now begin to answer my initial question, "Can an atheist be moral?" Now, ethics can prescribe some goods and make manifest some aims of action without demanding of a man the knowledge of God's existence. Aquinas in *ST* I-II, q. 94, a. 2, after having fixed the first principle of practical reason – *bonum est faciendum et prosequendum, et malum vitandum* ["the good is to be done and pursued, and evil is to be avoided"] – recognizes some very general human aims, correlated to fundamental inclinations. In order to understand some of these aims, a man doesn't require any knowledge of God's existence: for we are dealing with aims such as self-preservation (an aim that all the beings have in common); the union of a male with a female, the procreation and the education of the children (aims that man has in common with all the animals); the social life (an aim that is exclusive to human beings, because[5] animals are not social beings, but at the most merely gregarious); the

---

3   See B. Williams, *Ethics and the Limits of Philosophy* (London: Fontana Press, 1985), chapter 1.

4   See G. Abbà, *Lex et virtus. Studi sull'evoluzione della dottrina morale di san Tommaso d'Aquino* (Rome: LAS, 1983). Abbà amends other interpretations about the object of Aquinas' ethical thought, such as R. Guindon, *Bèatitude et théologie morale chez saint Thomas d'Aquin. Origines, interprétation* (Ottawa, 1956); O. H. Pesch, *Das Gesetz. I-II, 90-105* (Graz-Heidelberg: Deutsche Thomasausgabe 13, 1977); W. Kluxen, *Philosophische Ethik bei Thomas von Aquin* (Mainz: Grünevald, 1964).

5   See *In politicorum libris*, I, 1.

knowledge of truth (another aim exclusive to human beings, because the animal only knows what is useful and useless, and does not question the truth of things apart from their usefulness[6]).

Despite these inclinations being in general available even to the atheist, the last two aims that are exclusive to human beings receive from Aquinas a specification that requires the knowledge of God in order to be realized: to know the truth and to live in common means for a man to know the truth about God, as the most important thing, and to live absolutely in society with Him.

### Ethics and *ordo amoris*

Moreover, a man encounters many goods, and a virtuous man must hierarchically order them. Now, virtue is the *habitus* which improves the appetitive human dimension.[7] Despite some intellectualist passages, according to Aquinas *bonitas vel malitia moralis principaliter in voluntatis consistit*;[8] being good depends on the will, because human acts, in order to be moral, must be willed acts[9] and *quilibet habet bona voluntatem, dicitur bonus, in quantum habet bonam voluntatem; quia per voluntatem utitur omnibus quae sunt in nobis*.[10] In this sense Aquinas says that the will is the main part of a man: *voluntas hominis,[...] est potissimum in homine*.[11] So the place of virtue is the will and every principle of human behavior that stands under will's control.[12]

It is also true that virtue is the *bonum rationis*, involving the moderation of the passions and of the rational ordering of the operations of the appetitive dimension of man. According to Aquinas, every passion and every operation originates in and participates in love.[13] If all that is true, it is now possible to make a very important equivalence between two definitions of virtue: virtue as a realization of *bonum rationis* (which is the preferred formulation of Aquinas) is indeed equivalent to virtue as *ordo amoris* (a formulation which Aquinas adopts from Augustine[14]). Such an equivalence helps us understand that Thomistic ethics hinges on the primacy of love.

Actually, virtue is a sort of affection that is connatural with the good,[15] it is

---

6    *Ibidem.*

7    *ST.*, I-II, q. 58, a. 3.

8    *Ibid.*, q. 34, a. 4.

9    *Ibid.*, q. 74, a. 1: *cum autem proprium sit actuum moralium quod sint voluntarii.*

10   *Ibid.*, I, q. 5, a. 4, ad 3.

11   *Ibid.*, II-II, q. 34, a. 1.

12   *Ibid.*, I-II, q. 56, a. 3: *subiectum vero habitus qui simpliciter dicitur virtus, non potest esse nisi voluntas, vel aliqua potentia secundum quod est mota a voluntate.*

13   *In II Sent.*, d. 27, q. 1, a. 3; *In De Div. Nom.*, c. IV, l. IX, n. 401.

14   See *De Moribus Ecclesiae contra Manicheos*, c. 15, or *De Civ. Dei*, XV, 22.

15   *ST*, I-II, q. 59, a. 4: *virtus moralis perficit appetitivam partem animae ordinando ipsam in bonum rationis.*

a sort of orientation of the affectivity[16] so that it corresponds to the order of reason. If all this is correct, and if every passion and every operation of the appetites starts from love, and if moral virtue is essentially a particular explication of appetitive acts,[17] it is easy to infer that virtue, achieving the *bonum rationis*, and so achieving the regulation of passions and operations, achieves also the *ordo amoris*, the order of love – the regulation of love – that is the motive principle of every appetitive movement.

As Aquinas writes incidentally, we can say that virtue is the order of love because this order is precisely its aim, its purpose, and towards this aim it is directed and in this aim it is realized.[18] Any virtue requires a well ordered affection and, on the other hand, love is the root of every affection;[19] likewise, disordered love is implicit in every evil act.[20] So virtue is "the rectification by practical reason of the fundamental operating principle of human acts that is love. [...] Thanks to this regulation, love takes the good, worthy and right form for a man."[21] Again according to Aquinas, who cites the concise statement of Augustine:[22] *recta voluntas est bonus amor, et perversa voluntas est malus amor.*[23]

Even more precisely, the *ordo amoris* is realized whenever a man loves the goods:

> \* corresponding to the place they occupy in the hierarchy of value, that means following their specific value; and:

> \* corresponding to the way they must be loved, that is when they must be loved, with the intensity they required to be loved, and in the circumstances in which they must be loved.[24]

Goods are indeed many and various and of different dignities, so the problem is to order the desire, the affections and the passions that the goods arouse. In this way, aims give content; virtues give form to inclinations, to desires, to

---

16    *Ibid.*, II-II, q. 108, a. 2.

17    *Ibid.*, I-II, q. 56, a. 2, ad 3: *essentialiter in appetendo virtus moralis consistit.*

18    *Ibid.*, I-II, q. 55, a. 1, ad 4: *virtus dicitur ordo vel ordinatio amoris, sicut id ad quod est virtus: per virtutem enim ordinatur amor in nobis.*

19    *Ibid.*, q. 62, a. 2, ad. 3: *dicitur quaelibet virtus esse ordo amoris in quantum ad quamlibet cardinalium virtutum requiritur ordinata affectio: omnis autem affectionis radix et principium est amor.*

20    *Ibid.*, II-II, q. 125, a. 2: *amor ordinatus includitur in qualibet virtute, quilibet enim virtuosus amat proprium bonum virtutis; amor autem inordinatus includitur in quolibet peccato.* See also AugustinE, *De Mor.*, l. I, c. 15, n. 25.

21    G. Abbà, *Felicità, vita buona e virtù*, p. 61.

22    *De Civ. Dei*, XIV, 7.

23    *ST*, I-II, q. 26, a. 3, ad 3.

24    *In Ethic.*, l. 2, c. 6.

affections and to passions; form means order, the order required so that in every choice desire can be determined to its objects in a congruent way.

The last criterion of such an order, that is the last criterion of morality, must be the last aim of human life, to which the *finis proximus* of all virtue is ordered, because the goodness or malice of the will depends on the ultimate end. All the goods that a man desires, as ordered to and consistent with the ultimate end, are sought after rightly.[25] Now, since the ultimate end of human inclinations is communion with God, it is obvious that the totality of the acts of the will must be directed towards a last single end, that is God, and towards the other goods insofar as they are ordered to the ultimate end: a human act is good and virtuous when it is consistent with the love of God. Aquinas says, for example: *quodlibet humanum opus rectum est et virtuosum quando regulae divinae dilectionis concorda* (*In duo praecepta caritatis*, II, 1138). The will is right only in this way, that is, only if *amat quidquid amat sub ordinem ad Deum*,[26] otherwise it is evil.[27] So the human will is good if it is addressed to the supreme good that is God.[28]

In this way, the drama of freedom and the meaning of life is the duty to order love so that it is directed towards the true, authentic, ultimate end, in such a way that to God's love, which condescending to creation, there corresponds an ascending and rational love orienting creatures to God and to those who are loved by Him. In fact, when we love somebody we actually love the things that the beloved wishes, as long as these things are not evil; and in loving God, we cannot love evil, for God can want nothing but the good, since He is the supreme Wisdom and the supreme Good.

With these statements, the role of God in Thomistic ethics is already partly explained: God is the main aim of human inclinations and He is the criterion to order the aims hierarchically and to achieve the *ordo amoris*.

### Ethics' ultimate end and *Delectatio*

But an essential element is still missing. I have tried to explain that the ethics of Aquinas is oriented to an ultimate end, differing in this way from the primarily legalistic formulations of modern ethics. I have asserted that this ultimate end is God, but I still have to explain why this is the case.

Aquinas adopts a process of elimination to identify the man's ultimate end (*ST* I-II, q. 2). One after another wealth, honor, glory, power, pleasure, etc., are

---

25  *C. G.*, IV, c. 95: *bona quaecumque aliquis vult in ordine ad bonum finem, bene vult: mala autem quaecumque in ordine ad malum finem, male vult.*

26  *ST.*, I-II, q. 4, a. 4.

27  *In II Sent.*, d. 38, q. 1, sol.

28  *Ibid.*, q. 19, a. 9: *Requiritur ergo ad bonitatem humanae voluntatis, quod ordinetur ad summum bonum, quod est Deus.*

excluded from being identified with *beatitudo*. Here I will concentrate only on pleasure or *delectatio* and the reasons why it cannot be the ultimate end.

Is it not true that it is senseless to ask somebody why he wants to have pleasant experiences, and that for this reason pleasure has the character of the ultimate end, that is, something that is desired for itself and not for other purposes? In order to answer this question, we need to study the *delectatio*. Now, according to Aristotle,[29] as Aquinas explains, the *delectatio* is the result of an un-obstructed connatural operation.[30] An un-obstructed operation is indeed one that achieves its own object. So an un-obstructed connatural operation is nothing but a connatural operation which achieves a connatural good.[31] In this way, the *delectatio* is always the result of the operation because this operation achieves the connatural good, which means that the *delectatio* is mainly caused by the presence of the connatural good.[32] In other words, the agent has experience of the *delectatio* because, at the given moment (or in hope, or in memory), he has a good. So the *delectatio* is not a psychic condition independent of its content, but it follows the achievement of the object of the act. In other words, the will can attain the *delectatio* only because it achieves the desired good, intentionally or in reality.[33]

Now, if satisfaction is not a condition independent of the contents by which it is produced, if it is never a blind experience in regard to the good that produces it, its various shades, its different intensities, and its distinct degrees depend on the different content of the goods to which man is related.[34] Moreover, within every sphere of *delectationes* there will be as many possible *delectationes* as the possible objects and relations to them. But this is precisely why the *delectatio* cannot be the ultimate end, but it is what follows the achievement of the ultimate end.[35]

## The *Amor-Delectatio* connection

I will now try to explain the fundamental connection between *amor* and *delectatio*. According to Aquinas, joy is always a corollary of love, because a lover

---

29  *De Anima*, 1, 1.
30  *ST*, I-II, q. 31, a. 1: *quando constituitur res in propria operatione connaturali et non impedita, sequitur delectatio.*
31  *ST*, I-II, q. 31, a. 5.
32  *ST*, q. 31, a. 1.
33  *ST*, I-II, q. 2, a. 6, ad 1: *delectatio est appetibilis propter aliud, idest propter bonum, quod est delectationis obiectum, et per consequens est principium eius […] ex hoc enim delectatio habet quod appetatur, quia est quies in bono desiderato.*
34  In this way, Aquinas makes a distinction between sensible pleasure, which is related to the attainment of the sensible operations' objects, and spiritual joy, which is connected to the attainment of spiritual operations' objects, *ST*, I-II, q. 31, aa. 2-3.
35  *ST*, I-II, q. 2, a. 6: *nec ipsa delectatio quae consequitur bonum perfectum, est ipsa essentia beatitudinis; sed quoddam consequens ad ipsam sicut per se accidens.*

becomes appeased in his loved object,[36] and love is *causa delectationis.*[37] Actually (and human experience testifies to this), one could say that the activities that we perform for affection are joyful, even when they are hard and difficult.[38] But we seek a more precise anthropological explanation of this.

We have just said that *delectatio* is the result of a connatural operation that achieves a connatural aim. Now, even apart from identifying men's connatural aims, we can say that what is connatural is exactly the object of love.[39] Then, if we really consider the connatural good directed to that personal agent that is man, we clearly understand that it can only be a person, and moreover that Person who possesses the most ontological perfection in the universe.[40] But again, it is love that expresses itself in interpersonal communication: transcending the accidental qualities of the other person (qualities that can be similarly present in other subjects), it reaches to his personal, substantial center, which is unique and unrepeatable. *Amor amicitiae* achieves the other, apprehending it as an irreplaceable person, and only in a second moment it considers the psychophysical accidental qualities that are related to him. On the contrary, *amor concupiscentiae* reduces the other to a bundle of accidental and reproducible qualities, which may attach to the person, who remains at a "second level," and whose value is reduced to merely supporting such qualities as stir up emotion and passions.

Moreover, the best way to attain one thing is to identify oneself with it and to live its life without destroying it. But this function is proper to *amor amicitiae*, that is *vis estatica*, which projects towards the beloved, and *vis unitiva*, which establishes a communion with him. Now we start to understand the connection between *amor* and *delectatio*: love is the operation that has as an object that which is connatural to men, and *amor amicitiae* is the operation that achieves an object in the most perfect way[41]

But it also seems possible to say something else. A man is indeed open to the infinite, *omnium capax.*[42] That means that human nature is essentially characterized by openness, and it is a nature constitutively projected towards a union with every thing. So love not only has an object connatural to man and achieves its object in a more perfect way than every other operation, but also seems to be the operation that is above all connatural to man, because, being *vis estatica*, it is the expression and the connatural realization of a nature projected towards the

---

36    *ST*, I-II, q. 4, a. 3.

37    *Ibid.*, I-II, q. 100, a. 9, ad 3.

38    *In duo praecepta caritatis*, III, 1143: *etiam adversa et difficilia suavia videntur amanti.*

39    *ST*, I-II, q. 27, a. 1.

40    *ST*, I, q. 29, a. 3: *persona significat id quod est perfectissimum in tota natura.*

41    *ST*, I-II, q. 32, a. 3, ad 3: *omne enim amatum fit delectabile amanti: eo quod amor est quaedam unio vel connaturalitas amantis ad amatum.*

42    *De Ver.* q. 24, a. 10.

outside, and, being *vis unitiva*, it is the expression and connatural realization of a nature that can, in some way, join all things and establish communion with them.

Therefore: 1) the more love's explication is perfect and not prevented, the more it causes *delectatio*; 2) the stronger is love, the more intense is the *delectatio*.[43]

We can indeed understand that joy is a reflection of love if we reverse the question. We can now ask: When is a man unhappy? When his existence is characterized by true loneliness: a man who is really alone is dreadfully unhappy.[43] But in order to remedy the loneliness it is not enough to live among other people, because a man can be alone also among a crowd (as Kierkegaard explains very well). If a man has superficial interpersonal relationships he is not able to remedy the ontological loneliness that is typical of his constitutively open nature. Therefore, he must instead enrich his inner world, opening it to others and achieving interpersonal communion. This latter can be gained by *amor amicitiae*, which ecstatically projects the agent towards the other and, in this way, allows the agent to transcend his accidental qualities and to penetrate into his ontological core, making an identification, so that he can live the same life of the other. On the other hand, *amor concupiscentiae* does not remedy the ontological loneliness of man, and does not enable interpersonal communion, because the *exstasis* produced by it is only incipient and incomplete. The movement of the agent is centripetal, a movement of consumption and not of communion, and it closes him within the confining walls of the self. The agent not only excludes himself from accessing the personal and intimate center of the other, he precludes himself from even recognizing the other as a person, because he exploits the other as a thing.[45]

But then, if what we have said is true, if joy is the subjective reflection of love that produces inter-personal communion, then one who performs only acts of *amor concupiscentiae* excludes himself from joy, because only *amor amicitiae* is *vis ecstatica* and *unitiva*, while with *amor concupiscentiae* the agent only carries out a praxis of assimilation, not of communion; a praxis characterized by closure and not by aperture. The ecstatic movement of *amor concupiscentiae* only returns to the agent himself.

Therefore, *amor concupiscentiae* can be, in a given moment, a source of sensible pleasure, because it somehow implies the satisfaction of some tendency of man's sensible nature; but it cannot be the source of spiritual joy, because

---

43  See *C. G.*, I, c. 102: *cum delectatio ex amore causatur, ubi est maior amor, est maior delectatio in consecutione boni.*

44  Aristotle offers a profound insight, but without focusing on it, when he says: "We think that a friend is one of the greatest goods, and that it is dreadful to live without friends and in loneliness", *EE*, VII, 1234b 32 - 1235a 2.

45  As in Hegelian master-slave dialectic.

this depends on a conformity with human nature in its totality, as a constitutively opened, personal nature.

Human experience testifies that even sensible satisfaction is doomed to diminish and fade progressively. In fact, in the long run, in such a praxis characterized by closure, we see an increasing reduction of sensible pleasure itself; we see a progressively decreasing satisfaction, along with a progressively increasing desire, which can degenerate into frustration and pathology.[46] This is the psychology of addiction, for which we can now suggest an explanation: this kind of reiterating praxis characterized by closure is no longer occasional, but becomes a pattern of behavior progressively producing an *habitus*,[47] a second nature. This self-enclosed second nature directly conflicts with the openness of primary human nature, a nature which itself includes the sensible dimension. Man is a substantial union of two co-principles, body and soul, and therefore the sensible and spiritual levels interact and influence each other. Thus, in the end, the conflict between the two natures affects even sensible satisfaction.

### God as ethics' ultimate end

The constituent dependence of the *delectatio* on its contents, and the proportionality between the ontological quality of the content and the degree of the *delectatio*, have many consequences. Indeed, we have already seen that the fullest *delectatio* (if we don't aim at it directly[48]) can only be experienced if our actions have as content the highest object which it is possible to achieve. Moreover, one must argue that only the qualitatively highest object, the exceedingly perfect object (assuming it to be achievable), can have as a corollary a complete *delectatio*, which leaves nothing unsatisfied.

However, Aquinas develops an observation derived from experience, which is valid not only for pleasure but for the other failed candidates for the role of ultimate end: when we do achieve and possess it we do not appreciate it and we desire other things; that is, desire is never satisfied by it.[49] In other words, the experience of disillusionment is relevant to them all, even in their successful attainment. Frustration inevitably accompanies the fulfilment of an aim which is not the ultimate end but for which we were longing as if it had been the ultimate end. Upon getting what we wanted, we have the feeling that we did not get

---

46   See V. Frankl, *Theorie und Therapie der Neurosen* (München-Basel: UTB, 1975).

47   In fact, the *habitus* is an inclination to some acts which is acquired through a repetition of acts.

48   It is the paradox of happiness: to achieve happiness we must not research it directly, see G. Samek Lodovici, *La felicità del ben., Una rilettura di Tommaso d'Aquino* (Milan: Vita e Pensiero, 2002), pp. 179-183.

49   *ST*, I-II, q. 2, a. 1. Aquinas here quotes *Gv.*, 4, 13: "who drinks this water will be thirsty again."

what we really wanted.[50] So eventually we consider as relative or intermediate an aim that for some time we perceived as absolute and ultimate.

We can identify three possible negative consequences of this experience, three different attitudes:

- despair, in which a chain of disappointments leads the agent to infer that every hope of satisfaction is nonsensical.

- resignation, when the agent renounces complete satisfaction and is content with partial satisfactions.

- fanaticism, when the agent is agonizingly committed to increasing the partial satisfactions, trying by them to substitute for total satisfaction.[51]

Each attitude should be carefully considered. But here we intend to highlight a fourth consequence, which has a positive nature: the epiphany of the infinite good in the desire of each finite good. In fact, when we experience disappointment, we understand that this, far from pushing us into sadness because of man's insatiability, must be considered, according to Aquinas, in an optimistic way, as the evidence that the happiness which suits the spiritual level of human beings is another one. Then we perceive that man desires all what he wants, under the influence of the ultimate end,[52] and that the chain of disappointments is not aroused just from the nature of one or another finite good, but originates from our having forgotten the partiality that each finite good has in common insofar as finite.[53]

At this point we understand that when we were desiring the finite good, we were desiring something else too. So we discover that human conscience is the *symbolic* place where we deal with the finite nature of things, but we also perceive that there is something infinite, and we know consequently that every

---

50    Aristotle had just told about pleasure that: "everyone research a pleasure. But, perhaps, not the pleasure that he believes or he should say to research", *EN*, VII, 1153b 30. This argument is also the theme of Blondel, *L'action. Essai d'une critique de la vie et d'une science de la pratique* (Paris:F. Alcan, 1893).

51    See, for example, the phenomenology of the aesthetic stadium depicted by Kierkegaard, where man continuously consumes a material whose value he is unable to appreciate really. It is clear that the agent is here in search of, as Hegel would say, "a bad infinite," because it is a quantitative infinite instead of a qualitative infinite.

52    *ST*, I-II, q. 1, a. 6: *necesse est quod omnia quae homo appetit, appetat propter ultimum finem.*

53    It is also recognized by Nietzsche: "every pleasure desires eternity, desires profound, profound eternity", in *Also sprach Zarathustra. Ein Buch für Alles und Keinen,* Italian version *Così parlò Zarathustra. Un libro per tutti e per nessuno* (Milan: Adelphi, 1968), p. 278.

54    To see things precisely, also aesthetic experience, which, according to Kant, should

finite good is a symbolic anticipation of the infinite good.[54] At this point the inference arising from experience meets the metaphysical deduction in an almost inevitable conclusion. In fact, according to Aquinas, the good brings to perfection the thing that aims at it, and it can be so because of its suitability for the agent himself. It is clear that this suitability is just a correspondence to the specific nature of each being, to his essence.[55] The specific virtual transcendental nature of human mind and of will, their potentially infinite openness, consequently cannot be filled by a finite content, by a finite good. No created good can be the object of *beatitudo* because no created good can be *bonum perfectum quod totaliter quietat appetitum*.[56] Since each creature is not good in itself but is a participated good, it follows that the human will can be gratified only by God: *solus Deus voluntatem hominis implere potest*.[57]

---

be an experience of fulfilment, on the contrary produces a sense of nostalgia, so admirably expressed by S. Weil: "A beautifull thing does not contain anything but itself. We go towards it without kwowing what can we ask of it, and this thing offers us its existence. When we posses it, we do not want anything more; but, at the same time, we desire something more, without kwowing what. We would like to go beyond, behind the beauty, but that is only superficial. It is like a mirror which gives back our desire of good. It is a sphinx, an enigma, a painfully irritating mystery." S. Weil, *Attente de Dieu* (Paris: Arthème Fayard, 1966), Italian version *Attesa di Dio* (Milan: Rusconi, 1972), p. 132. In another passage: "in this world we feel as strangers, aimless, in exile; like Ulysses, who awoke in an unknown country, where the sailors had transported him while he was sleeping, and felt Ithaca's desire lacerating his soul", *Ibid.*, p. 144.

55 *ST.*, I-II, q. 18, a. 5: *unicuique enim rei est bonum quod convenit ei secundum suam formam.*

56 *ST,* I-II, q. 2, a. 8.

57 *Ibid.* See AugustinE, *Conf.* I, 1: *quia fecisti nos ad te et inquietum est cor nostrum donec requiescat in te.* The ethimology of Latin *desiderium* just allude to the final object of it, because the word is composed by privative "de" and by "sidera", so that it expresses that Heaven is the definitive fulfilment. See also Pascal's penetrating consideration, *Pensées*, Italian version *Pensieri, opuscoli, lettere* (Milano: Rusconi, 1978), n. 370, p 535: "every man seeks happiness, without exceptions; though they use different means, they all aim to this end. [...]. The will does not take a step to any other object. It is the reason of every action of men, including those who go to hang themselves. But, after so long a number of years, no person has gained, without the faith, the end to which everyone continuously aims. Everyone complains: princes, subjects, nobles, plebeians, old men, young people, strong and weak persons; learned men, ignorant persons; healty and sick men; persons of every country, of every time; of every age, of every conditions. Such a long, continuous, and uniform witness should well convince us of our incapacity to reach the good with our own strength; but this witness does not teach us enough. Nothing is so equal to something else as to exclude some small difference; and for this reason we expect that next time we will not be frustrated, unlike other times. In this way, the present

GIACOMO SAMEK LODOVICI

## Summary

In this paper I have tried to show the role of God in Aquinas's ethics. First, I have explained that, unlike modern ethics, Aquinas's ethics emphasizes self-fulfilment and happiness as its aims. Then I have explained that ethics indicates the aims of the inclinations and that man's specific inclinations are only fulfilled in God. Furthermore, I have argued that the virtuous man orders his aims hierarchically, realizing the *ordo amoris*, only if he orders them according to God's love. Then I have explained why God is the ultimate end of ethics, first pointing out the connection between *delectatio* and the ultimate end, and the connection of *amor* with *delectatio*; then, reflecting inductively on the feeling of disappointment and deductively on human nature, a nature which is open without limit, I have concluded that only communion with God suits man's desire for the infinite and can be the ultimate end of human nature, whose attainment never disappoints.

---

time does not satisfy, the experience deceives us, and passing from one misfortune to another, it leads us to death, which is its eternal climax. What does this avidity and this incapacity show apart from the fact [...] that man tries in vain to attain happiness with everything around him, asking the help of the absent things that present things are unable to give, while everything is incapable, because that infinite abyss can only be filled up by an infinite and immutable object, that is God?"

# Who Made the Law? God, Ethics, and the Law of Nature

## Robert A. Gahl, Jr.

### Killing God by Extirpating Morality

The famous first chapter of Alasdair MacIntyre's *After Virtue* offers a "disquieting suggestion," a creative thought experiment, inspired by Walter Miller's classic novel of science fiction, *A Canticle for Leibowitz*. With this hypothesis of an imaginary, global environmental catastrophe, MacIntyre provokes his reader to view moral language from a new perspective so as to more easily perceive the depths of change effected by modern moral philosophy. The change in the language by which we express ourselves reflects a change in our very self-understanding. One of the principal theses of *After Virtue* is that: "Modern moral utterance and practice can only be understood as a series of fragmented survivals from an older past."[1]

In chapter nine, the central and cardinal chapter of *After Virtue*, entitled with a question comparable to our conference title, "Nietzsche or Aristotle?," MacIntyre offers an historical anecdote which provides a fascinating sociological illustration of the relationship between moral law and authority, divine or otherwise. The great explorer Captain Cook records in the journal of his third voyage the first discovery of the Polynesian word *taboo* by English speakers.

> The English seamen [no, there were no female sailors on board] had been astonished at what they took to be the lax sexual habits of the Polynesians and were even more astonished to discover the sharp contrast with the rigorous prohibition placed on such conduct as that of men and women eating together. When they enquired why men and women were prohibited from eating together, they were told that the practice was taboo. But when they enquired further what the word *taboo* meant, they could get little further information. Clearly *taboo* did not simply mean *prohibited*, for to say that

---

1   *After Virtue*. Notre Dame, IN: University of Notre Dame Press, 2nd edition, 1984, pp. 110–11.

something – person, or practice, or theory – is *taboo* is to give some particular sort of reason for its prohibition.[2]

On account of the discoveries made in successive anthropological studies, we
now know that taboo was a remnant from the Polynesian past, whose meaning
had been lost.

MacIntyre, always a promoter of productive thought experiments, suggests
that we imagine what modern analytic philosophers, emotivists, or neo-Kantians
would have to say about the meaning and usage of taboo. Moore would have
considered it the name used to designate a non-natural property. Emotivists
would define taboo as "I disagree with this, do so as well." A third interpretation, upon noticing that no one in society questioned taboo, and that everyone
took it for granted, would have seen *taboo* as the Polynesian expression for a
universalizable, imperative prohibition.[3]

In our study of the relationship between God and natural law, I would suggest that we also consider how the twentieth century legal scholar H.L.A. Hart
would have classified Polynesian taboo within his theory of jurisprudence.
Perhaps he would have concluded that taboo represents a set of primary rules.
The Nietzschean postmodernist would offer a more radical response to Captain
Cook's discovery. Taboo is simply a mask behind which the speaker hides his
will to power. And in fact, as MacIntyre pointed out, Nietzsche had a Hawaiian
predecessor, not a philosopher but a king and an eminently practical man. Forty
years after Captain Cook's discovery in 1819, King Kamehameha II decreed the
abolition of taboo for all of Hawaii. And life went on in the Pacific islands just
as before the king's historic decree.

We have seen how the Mooreian, the emotivist, the neo-Kantian, the positivist analytic legal scholar, and the Nietzschean would have viewed taboo. What
about the Thomist? Always respectful of sources and tradition, the Thomist
would assume that Polynesian taboo must be an historic relic, cut off from its
past, and that these prohibitions were once based on good reasons and, perhaps,
the legislation of a sovereign authority. The Thomistic analysis of MacIntyre's
antidotal anecdote looks much like the more explicative conclusion of empirical anthropological research.

The Polynesian experience of taboo and its abolition helps manifest distinctions within our moral and legal vocabulary. Allow me to begin my brief analysis of moral and legal vocabulary with expressions of prohibition, because these
are simpler than the positive affirmations of moral obligation. Human experience of prescription probably first involves the perception of the linguistic
expression of prohibitions. Even if some with more experience raising children
might object by holding that babies hear commandments like "go to sleep" and

2    *After Virtue*, p. 111
3    *After Virtue*, p. 112

"finish your milk," before prohibitions like "don't pull mommy's hair" or "don't throw your food," nevertheless it has got to be the case that positive affirmations that recommend action are more nuanced and circumstance-dependent than prohibitions. Prohibitions, therefore, permit more straightforward analysis. When we say that someone ought not to do something, we may mean to entail a combination of any or all of the following fifteen significations–and perhaps some others..[4]

1. If you do that you will have acted in a way different from common social expectations.
2. I don't want you to do that.
3. If you do that you are going to suffer some negative consequences.
4. If you do that you will hurt someone (either yourself, someone else, or both).
5. Someone whom you habitually obey has commanded that you not do that.
6. Someone who is established in power has commanded that you not do that.
7. Someone who is established in authority has commanded that you not do that.
8. If you do that you are going to be punished.
9. If you do that you will have acted wrongly or wickedly.
10. If you do that you will not receive the reward or prize that you pursue.
11. If you do that you will have acted in a way contrary to your nature.
12. If you do that you will have acted in a way offensive to tradition or to your ancestors.
13. If you do that (and someone were to notice) you will lose honor and respect.
14. If you do that you will have acted unreasonably.
15. If you do that you will have acted against the will of God.

Earlier, I mentioned how Hart might have characterized Polynesian taboo because Hart's view of law and morality has – to use an expression from fluid dynamics – a much smaller profile than the Thomistic view of law and morality. Hart's carries much less metaphysical baggage, or – depending on your point of view – equipment. He has cut down the ontological requirements for law to the point that, although he considers it unusual, Hart acknowledges the possibility of a morality whose rules are "generally held by those who subscribe to them to be in no way preferable to alternatives and of no intrinsic importance."[5]

---

4    For my analysis of the significations of prohibitions I have been inspired by MacIntyre's *Against the Self-Images of the Age: Essays on Ideology and Philosophy*, in which he examines the major features of the debates of the early second half of the twentieth century regarding the meaning of "ought."

Polynesian taboo would therefore be a viable, although strange, form of morality for Hart. On Hart's account of morality, a prohibition may be considered moral if it satisfy just one of the significations mentioned above – that is, the second signification: "If you do that you will have acted in a way different from common social expectations." All the other meanings drop out from his understanding of morality. Hart offers hypothetical examples of such unusually "thin" morality. He writes that it is possible to attach specifically moral importance to driving on the left, instead of the right of the road, entirely aside from the legal conventions currently in practice. Hart's concept of morality is so entirely untouched by the need for reasonableness, order, hierarchy, authority, reward, punishment, and so on, that he can affirm that it is possible to hold a view of morality according to which it would be wrong to break a promise made before two witnesses but just fine to break a promise made before only one.[6] Although such moral beliefs would be quite different than those held by Hart and contemporary Western society, they may still be classified as moral according to his minimalist account of morality.

In order to perform his careful analysis of legal terminology, Hart has stepped back into a Rawlsian sort of "original position" in order to consider morality and law without any reference to inherent intelligibility, authority, or potential human perfection. For Hart, law need not be based on any metaphysical or natural order nor must it be promulgated by any sovereign authority endowed with particular power. He succeeds in supplanting all vestige of authoritative sovereignty constituted by any sort of "ontological" hierarchy. Although Hart does consider authority to be a necessary constituent for the development of primary rules into secondary, his notion of authority is, once again, designed to minimize the effects of ontological "drag." Hart observes that, historically, the legal has developed from the pre-legal through various stages: first the encoding of unwritten rules and then, more importantly, the "acknowledgement of reference to the writing or inscription as *authoritative*, i.e., as the *proper* way of disposing of doubts as to the existence of the rule. Where there is such an acknowledgement there is a very simple form of secondary rule: a rule for conclusive identification of the primary rules of obligation."[7] So, while his legal theory does include the recognition of a legislating authority, the determination and definition of the authority does not include competency, responsibility, or even the authority's existence, just recognition by the subjects of those rules that are seen as having emanated from the authority. For Hart, authority is not established, at least not primarily, on account of office or charge, such as king, senate, sergeant, bishop, teacher, or mother. Hart's notion of the sovereign lawgiver is so deeply depleted from the traditional notion that,

---

5     *The Concept of Law,* p. 229
6     *The Concept of Law*, p. 229
7     *The Concept of Law,* p. 94–95.

for Hart, the sovereign is constituted by the rules he emanates and by their "habitual" acceptance by the sovereign's subjects.[8]

Although I agree with John Rist's criticism of Lisska's *Aquinas's Theory of Natural Law*,[9] I nurture great sympathy for Lisska's effort to defend ethical naturalism in Aquinas. Nonetheless, I dare to quibble with a very small point in his contribution here, involving a, perhaps, over-generous reading of Hart's understanding of the human right to the protection against violence. Hart argues from the existence of positive law to the existence of something like natural law in the following fashion. If it were not for some more basic set of rules protecting us from gross aggression, then all other rules would be entirely ineffective. What would be the point of say, the laws prohibiting spitting on the sidewalks, smoking in Hesburgh Library or speeding on the Indiana turnpike if there were not already a socially accepted prohibition of murder? So, yes, the empirical reality of positive law can be used to argue back to a real theory of natural law. But from an empirical description alone and without a metaphysics it is quite hard to develop a causal account of natural law.

Upon observing the achievement of his subtle distinctions used to trim down the cumbersome profile of traditional conceptions of law, Hart nearly gloats over his accomplishment. "Once we abandon the view that the foundations of a legal system consist in a habit of obedience to a legally unlimited sovereign and substitute for this the conception of an ultimate rule of recognition which provides a system of rules with its criteria of validity, a range of fascinating and important questions confronts us."[10] What better way to advance the Nietzschean pursuit of the death of God than by extirpating nearly all the features of traditional morality and legality from moral philosophy and jurisprudence? At that point, God has little room left in human life.

## Morality without Authority?

In Dostoevsky's *Brothers Karamazov*, Ivan claims "if there is no immortality, there is no virtue," and consequently, since for Ivan there is no God and no immortality, "everything is lawful." Jean Paul Sartre, while describing the existentialist's predicament, offered us the succinct and more quotable version of Ivan's conclusion in the following phrase. "The existentialist ...finds it extremely embarrassing that God does not exist, for there disappears with him all possibility of finding values in an intelligible heaven.... Dostoevsky once wrote, 'If God did not exist, everything would be permitted.'" In comparison to Ivan Karamazov, Sartre, the existentialist, is more pungent and more primitive.

Like Dostoevsky, Rist holds that without belief in God, no one, in fact, has

---

8    Ibid., p. 76
9    Rist, *Real Ethics,* p. 152–54
10   Ibid., p. 110

been able to effectively demonstrate the need to conform one's life to a consistent set of moral obligations. "The notion that God, if he exists can be bracketed out of an account of the nature of moral virtue and of human flourishing assuredly makes no sense."[11] Nonetheless, it is possible to assemble an impartial, even if fundamentally non-persuasive account of the moral life, without any reference to God. Many atheistic, or simply secularist, proposals for a moral philosophy have been advanced on foundational underpinnings such as the maximization of goods, dutiful obedience to universalizable moral imperatives, practical reasonableness, fulfillment of human nature, Stoic self-control, even the value of fostering and preserving fidelity in friendships. Some Thomists strongly advocate the rational persuasiveness of a secularist version of Aristotelian moral philosophy without any need to refer to the divine as a transcendent principle of order for the moral life. Such naturalist and non-theistic, secularist moral philosophies can indeed offer sound motives for virtuous action. They can supply us with quite a few, even the majority, of the fifteen propositions that I mentioned earlier to describe the significations of a prohibition. But is it possible to construct anything close to a sound and stable account of natural law without theism? And by theism, I mean some conceptual cognition of the divine, not a full-blooded, scientific theology.

For Thomists the problem of a secularist account of natural law is obvious. Aquinas defined law as "a work of reason, made and promulgated by a competent authority for the common good."[12] That law be caused and promulgated by an authority, is not unique to Aquinas. The need for promulgation in the definition of law is a commonplace throughout the history of legal philosophy. For instance, John Austin, a positivist quite distant from the metaphysical presuppositions of Aquinas, defines law as "the command of a sovereign backed by sanctions and habitually obeyed."[13] Unless you are a Kantian and therefore hold that one can give himself or herself the law, it is very difficult to imagine how one could be rationally subject to a law without recognizing that law as coming from an authority higher than oneself. Perhaps ridicule, of the sort famously used by Anscombe, is the best response to the idea of giving oneself the law. In *Modern Moral Philosophy* she wrote: " whatever you may do for yourself may be admirable; but it is not legislating. That legislation can be 'for oneself' I reject as absurd."[14]

---

11  See *Real Ethics,* 153; see also Rist's response to his critics in this volume.

12  *ST,* I-II, q. 90, a. 4: "Et sic ex quatuor praedictis potest colligi definitio legis, quae nihil est aliud quam quaedam rationis ordinatio ad bonum commune, ab eo qui curam communitatis habet, promulgata."

13  *The Province of Jurisprudence Determined.* 1832, reprint. New York: Noonday Press, 1954, quotation taken from Hittinger's Introduction to Heinrich Rommen's, *The Natural Law.* Indianapolis: The Liberty Fund, 1998, xxvii.

14  "Ethics, Religion and Politics," pp. 26–42 in *Modern Moral Philosophy.*

Moreover, to explain natural law as simply an exigency of nature does not seem to provide anything close to a fully persuasive reason to obey that exigency in all circumstances, time, and *place, "semper et pro semper,"* as John Paul II writes in *Veritatis Splendor*.[15] Nevertheless, John Finnis has described, if not defined, natural law without referring to any promulgator whatsoever. The most striking text of his I have found, and one of the most cryptic philosophical explanations I have ever encountered, is the following from the *Oxford Companion to Philosophy*.[16]

> **natural law.** *Moral standards which, on a long-dominant but now disfavoured type of account of morality, political philosophy, and law, can justify and guide political authority, make legal rules rationally binding, and shape concept formation in even descriptive social theory.*
>
> The sounder versions (e.g. of Plato, Aristotle, and Aquinas) consider morality 'natural' precisely because reasonable (in an understanding neither conseqentialist nor Kantian). Likewise, contemporary versions plead not guilty of the 'is-ought' fallacy: natural law's first (not yet specifically moral) principles identify basic reasons for action, basic human goods which are-to-be (ought to be) instantiated through choice. Practical knowledge of these presupposes, but is not deduced from, an 'is' knowledge of possibilities; full 'is' knowledge of human nature is partly dependent on, not premiss for, practical ('is-to-be') understanding of the flourishing (including moral reasonableness) of human individuals and communities.

In his more recent and more systematic book entitled *Aquinas,* Finnis offers Aquinas's definition of law but then proceeds to explain in his own words the "fundamental notion of law" as "a prescription of *reason*, by means of which rational and indeed conscientious and reasonable practical judgments about the needs of a complete community's common, public good, having been made and published by lawmakers, are understood and adopted by citizens as the *imperium* of their own autonomous, individual practical reason and will."[17] This explanation is certainly closer to that of Aquinas insofar as it includes explicit reference to the lawmaker. But also curiously distant from Aquinas's notion of law insofar as Finnis emphasizes that law is fundamentally understood as an imperium of the "autonomous ... reason and will" of the very subject.

While it may be possible to construct a secularist ethical theory that offers a rational and coherent, even if not complete account of morality, a theory of natural law is another question. According to all definitions of law, coherent with our experience, legal obligation entails obedience to the authoritative command of a superior. While an impartial account of ethics may be advanced

---

15    *VS* nos. 52&82.

16    Ted Honderich, Oxford University Press, 1995.

17    *Aquinas*, p. 258

without reference to God, to propose a natural law theory without some transcendent authority is not only impractical but absurd.

### God in Natural Law: Aquinas's Fundamental Option.

For Aquinas, natural law is, of course, a participation in the eternal law of God.
While the eternal law is eternally promulgated in God, through the Father's generation of the Eternal Word and in the Book of Life,[18] the natural law is caused
in the human by God through a participated illumination of the human intellect.[19]

Above I referred to the promulgation of the eternal law, even though it
might at first seem to be an ethereal theological topic unrelated to that of the
requirements for the promulgation of natural law. But, Aquinas raises an objection within his discussion of the eternal law that is most relevant to our discussion of the need to know the divine legislator in order to be legally subject to the
law of nature. How can eternal law satisfy the Thomistic definition of law if it
always existed? To whom could it have been eternally promulgated? Aquinas
responds to the second objection of q. 91, a. 1 by affirming that the eternal law
is eternally promulgated by word (*verbo*) and by writing (*scripto*). On God's
part, the promulgation is eternal, because the Eternal Word and the Scripture of
the Book of Life are eternal (fascinating implications for a narrative theology of
law, but no time or space for this right now). On the creature's part, the promulgation of the eternal law cannot be eternal.

Knowledge of the natural law and of its lawmaker is natural but not innate.
The human discovers the exigencies of nature through the experience of both
sensitive and rational desire and the satisfaction of those desires consequent
upon the attainment of their objects. To cognitively grasp particular goods is to
begin to understand the natural law. But such knowledge of particular goods is
insufficient for one to be subject to the law in accord with rational nature.
Human rationality includes the ability to order goods to a single end. It is only
once one can order everything towards the due end that the human enjoys the
use of reason. To have come to know that all other goods are for the sake of a
single and absolute good, that for which all others are desired, is to have come

---

18  *ST* I-II, 91, a.1, ad 2: "Ad secundum dicendum quod promulgatio fit et verbo et
    scripto; et utroque modo lex aeterna habet promulgationem ex parte Dei promulgan-
    tis, quia et verbum divinum est aeternum, et Scriptura libri vitae est aeterna. Sed ex
    parte creaturae audientis aut inspicientis, non potest esse promulgatio aeterna."

19  *ST* I-II, q. 91, a. 2: "signatum est super nos lumen vultus tui, domine, quasi lumen
    rationis naturalis, quo discernimus quid sit bonum et malum, quod pertinet ad nat-
    uralem legem, nihil aliud sit quam impressio divini luminis in nobis. unde patet
    quod lex naturalis nihil aliud est quam participatio legis aeternae in rationali crea-
    tura."

to know that the good life is required by the one absolute good and that attainment of the only good that can fully satisfy human desire requires the reasonable ordering of all others to it. Since such knowledge of the due end of human life includes understanding that the transcendent good and organizing principle puts moral demands upon us, such knowledge is, at least, very close to understanding that a superior authority, or even lawgiver, demands that our action conform to an ordering of ourselves and all else towards the end.

Careful examination of the final article of the *Treatise on Sin*, q. 89, a. 6, often called the fundamental option article, offers more detail regarding the kind of knowledge of the final end that is required for fully human action and thus, what we must know to be under the natural law as rational creatures. Q. 89, a. 6 asks whether venial sin can exist in a person with original sin alone. That is, if one can be in original sin, not have committed a mortal sin, but commit a venial one. In his response Aquinas explains that "it is impossible that venial sin be in someone with original sin but not mortal." He goes on to explain that if before reaching the age of reason one's lack of discretion excuses one from mortal sin, one is much more, "*multo magis*," excused from venial sin, if one were to commit something of that kind. And if one has already attained discretion, one is responsible, and therefore may not be excused from either venial or mortal sin. Aquinas then describes the dynamic of the first free act by asserting that use of reason entails the ability to deliberate about one's self and order one's self to the due end. Aquinas writes:"Should he order himself to the due end, through grace he obtains remission of original sin. On the other hand if he fails to order himself to the due end, acording to the discretional capacity of his age, he mortally sins, failing namely, 'to do what in him lies.'"

Aquinas's description of the requirements for the use of reason leaves no space for the possibility of morally good action without grace. If one reads the *Treatise on Law* within its proper context, one notices that no free human action may fulfill the requirements of the natural law without the aid of sanctifying grace. Granted, one may perform an act of some single virtue (considered specifically, not generally), but if one is habitually directed away from the due end, even an act of some particular virtue cannot be considered on the whole good, precisely because it does not lead to the end, even if it may dispose the agent to future conversion.

But q. 89, a. 6 is based on a theological thesis regarding the effects of original sin. Why should moral philosophy even consider the need for conversion to the due end? Any eudaimonistic moral philosophy coupled with a teleological view of human nature must include a rational determination of the human being towards the final end that perfects human nature.[20] If one's philosophical anthropology does not include something like a doctrine of original sin, that is, a

---

20   For a deep and persuasive account of the rational requirements for a unifying last

disorientation of the human being from birth, the determination towards the final end may not be described as a conversion, a moving away from something else for the sake of the final end, but it must still be a free and rational determination of the self towards the ultimate end.

What if the ultimate end were simply a vague and implicit notion of happiness? For Aquinas such a claim is unsustainable. The ordering of oneself to the end must be an act of volition, of love. As Aquinas shows in the disputed questions *De Veritate* q. 14, a. 11, while arguing for the necessity of explicit faith in order to be saved, *"(utrum) sit necessarium explicite credere,"* love cannot be implicit since the object of love must be a thing extrinsic to one's soul and subsisting in a particular. Even if one were raised in the woods among the wolves, Aquinas says that such a person must explicitly believe in God as his remunerator in order to be saved. Once again, we have to distinguish between the theological and philosophical elements of the argument. In *De Veritate*, Aquinas is considering the requirements for salvific faith within the context of theology. But his argumentation is nonetheless instructive for moral philosophy. The volitional determination of oneself for the highest good requires some knowledge of that good. You cannot love what you do not know. "Nihil volitum nisi praecognitum." In the order of being, the final end is of course God, the lawmaker, and our remunerator. In the order of knowing, the knowledge that the final end is the highest good gets us, at least, very close to knowing God as remunerator because if one comes to understand that everything else is for the sake of the highest good, then possession of the highest good must be worth withstanding any demand to forego possession of the particular goods here and now. In fact, it is for this reason that Aquinas proposes in the *Commentary on the Ethics* that it is the hope for the desired good that which causes courage to be capable of overcoming evil.[21] To act for the sake of the final end necessarily involves some kind of hope of achieving this goal. If the human acts in accord with the principles that are in him on account of his nature, he will achieve much more than that which nature desires. He will be justified and will receive the gift of sanctifying grace. In the response to the first objection in *De Veritate* q. 14, a. 11, Aquinas concludes with the encouraging claim that it is most certain – *"certissime est tenendum"* – that everyone has the sufficient means to come to know the final end as one's remunerator and therefore order one's life to the due end and receive sanctifying grace.[22] Either through interior inspiration,

---

end as the principle of hierarchy for an Aristotelian moral epistemology, see Daniel McInerny's contribution to this volume, as well as his *Difficult Good*, 2006.

21   See *In Sententia Libri Ethicorum, III, 15, 12:* "et ideo spes, cuius est tendere in bonum, est causa audaciae quae tendit in malum quod aggreditur."

22   "quod Deus ei vel per internam inspirationem revelaret ea quae sunt necessaria ad credendum, vel aliquem fidei praedicatorem ad eum dirigeret, sicut misit Petrum ad Cornelium, Act. X."

revelation, or through a preacher of the faith, God will reveal that which is necessary to believe.

Our conference is entitled with the question: "Ethics without God?" Although a partial and incomplete description of the moral life may be given without reference to God, no coherent theory of natural law may be sustained without some recognition of a divine principle and final end. Without relying on specifically theological argumentations based on faith in Christian revelation, the Thomistic philosopher can develop a coherent, rationally defensible, theistic account of the moral life and of the natural law that is capable of explaining many facets of the demands required within the human striving for happiness. But because of our predicament as children of Adam and Eve, the Thomistic theologian recognizes that a theistic philosophical account is not quite adequate for explaining our radical need for and the availabilty of the redeeming grace of the new law so as to fulfill the requirements and achieve the aims of the natural law and then much, much more beyond our natural desires.

# Hierarchy and Direction for Choice

## Daniel McInerny

This essay is a response to an invitation. Robert George has recently request-ed from "neo-scholastics" "a detailed account of how choosing in accordance with a principle of hierarchy is supposed to work across a set of cases."[1] George's invitation is put forward in a defense of what he calls "the incommen-surability thesis" and its role in giving direction to human choice. Put briefly, and quoting George, "[t]he incommensurability thesis states that basic values and their particular instantiations as they figure in options for choice cannot be weighed and measured in accordance with an objective standard of compar-ison."[2] This raises a crucial question. In the absence of an objective standard of comparison, how is non-arbitrary choice between basic goods possible? For George, it is possible because the very respect that is due to the incommensu-rability of the basic goods generates principles that objectively guide human action.

What reasons does George give for rejecting a natural hierarchy of human goods? First of all, it should be said that George does recognize certain natural hierarchies. Instrumental goods, he acknowledges, are subordinate to intrinsi-cally valuable goods; sensible goods are subordinate to intelligible goods; and a fuller realization of the good is to be preferred to a meager realization.[3] When George speaks of incommensurable "basic" goods, therefore, at issue is not these hierarchies but rather the set of intrinsically valuable, intelligible goods that together comprise human happiness. Similarly for the Thomist, the argu-ment for hierarchy principally concerns relationships between intrinsically valu-able human goods.

So why then does George reject a natural hierarchy of basic goods, and the making of moral judgments on the basis of such a hierarchy? The reason he gives is put in the context of the following example. Imagine a golfer faced with a decision between interrupting his best chance to break 80 and the

---

1  Robert P. George, *In Defense of the Natural Law* (Oxford University Press, 1999), Chapter 2, note 125, pp. 81–82.
2  Ibid., p. 93.
3  Ibid., pp. 93–94.

opportunity to rescue a child drowning in the water hazard on the adjacent fairway. Granted that the only moral choice for the golfer is to drop his club and try and rescue the child, the question is how this decision is reached. For George, what is clear is that the golfer does not make his decision by acknowledging that the basic good of "life" is objectively better than the basic good of "play." Why not? The answer is twofold: because *either* the notion of hierarchy places in jeopardy the common sense belief "that one ordinarily has no moral duty to forego one's ordinary pursuits, including playing golf, to devote oneself to life-saving or to join famine relief projects and other worthy lifesaving endeavors in far off places," *or* the notion of hierarchy fails to provide a principle on the basis of which to decide when choices for "life" are required and when they are not.[4] In other words, for George, either hierarchy forces us to fanatically reduce the value of lower goods in the hierarchy in favor of higher goods, and indeed the highest good, or it simply fails to do any work in telling us when choices in favor of a super-ordinate good are required. In either case, hierarchy seems hopeless in providing direction for choice, while the incommensurability thesis allows for the intrinsic choice-worthiness of basic goods even while it grounds the principles that would direct us at times to favor one basic good over another.

George is exactly right that the incommensurability thesis runs counter to what he calls the "neo-scholastic" – I would say principally Thomistic – understanding that the human good exists naturally as a hierarchical arrangement – a *duplex ordo* as Aquinas describes it in the first *lectio* of the *Commentary on the Ethics* – in which goods are ordered both to one another and to the absolutely ultimate end.[5] So in responding to George's invitation, what I aim to do in this essay is to provide an introduction, at least, to a Thomistic understanding of how the natural hierarchy of human goods provides direction for choice. In sum, I will be arguing that non-arbitrary choices between contending substantial, or intrinsically valuable, goods are only possible when one of the goods is seen either as a necessary or expedient means for the attainment of another and intrinsically more valuable good. For Aquinas, in any line of action what is obligatory in itself is the intrinsically valuable good, or end, and that which is for the sake of this end, the means, is obligatory on account of it, either by being necessary or expedient to the attainment of this end.[6] In determining, then, which of two or more choices is necessary or most expedient to the attainment

4    Ibid., p. 98.
5    "Invenitur autem duplex ordo in rebus. Unus quidem partium alicujus totius seu alicujus multitudinis adinvicem, sicut partes domus adinvicem ordinantur. *Alius* est ordo rerum in finem. Et hic ordo est principalior, quam primus. Nam, ut Philosophus dicit in undecimo Metaphysicorum, ordo partium exercitus adinvicem, est propter ordinem totius exercitus ad ducem." *In I Ethicorum*, lectio 1, no. 1.
6    See especially *ST* I-II q. 99, a. 1, and II-II q. 44, a. 1.

of an intrinsically superior end, deliberation must first discern the appropriate natural hierarchy of human goods.

Several important issues hang on whether the incommensurability or hierarchy thesis wins this debate. Most obvious is the issue of how to justify non-arbitrary choices between conflicting, substantial goods. But analogous to this is the issue of how to justify non-arbitrary choices between entire life-plans. Would I have non-arbitrary reasons for becoming a butcher, baker, or candlestick maker? This latter issue touches upon a further question. If there is indeed a natural hierarchy of human goods, does this imply that there is one and only one "right" way of living a human life? Where in the argument for hierarchy, in other words, do considerations of wish, talent and temperament come in?

The debate between incommensurability and hierarchy also raises the question of how to adjudicate between the *bonum mihi* and the *bonum commune*, the good that is a personal good for me here and now and the good that by nature is shared with those with whom I live in community. Is there a hierarchical ordering between these two kinds of good, or are they themselves incommensurable considerations of human agents?[7]

But the most important – because the most fundamental – issue raised by this debate concerns the unity of the human good. For Thomists this comes down to the question of the ultimate end, of happiness. Thomists understand the ultimate end to have several analogous senses, the most primary of which identify the ultimate end with God. For the Thomist, God is the *principium* of the hierarchy of goods, and thus God ultimately unifies the human good by providing the ultimate direction for choice.[8] Defenders of incommensurability, by contrast, understand happiness solely in an inclusivistic sense; that is, as the name we give to that miscellany of incommensurable basic goods that give us satisfaction. While the inclusivist view does well in capturing our sense of the multiplicity of the human good, it seems to do less well in showing us how the collection of incommensurables amounts to anything more than the sum of various parts. Such a multiform view of human fulfillment has serious implications for a unified conception of the human person.[9]

---

7    The incommensurability between what he calls "agent-relative" and "agent-neutral" reasons for action is defended by Mark C. Murphy in *Natural Law and Practical Rationality* (Cambridge University Press, 2001), esp. p. 186.

8    *ST* II-II q. 26, a. 1: "prius et posterius dicitur secundum relationem ad aliquod principium. Ordo autem includit in se aliquem modus prius et posterius. Unde oportet quod ubicumque est aliquod principium, sit etiam aliquis ordo...."

9    A problem discussed by Hittinger, *A Critique of the New Natural Law Theory*, Chapter 2, especially pp. 73ff.; and Benedict M. Ashley, O.P., "What is the End of the Human Person? The Vision of God and Integral Human Fulfillment," in Luke Gormally, ed., *Moral Truth and Moral Tradition: Essays in Honor of Peter Geach and Elizabeth Anscombe* (Dublin: Four Courts Press, 1994), pp. 68–96.

I want to address these issues from a Thomistic point of view in the following way. George has asked, in particular, for a detailed account of how choice in the context of hierarchy works across a set of cases. I believe it would be a mistake, however, to get down to cases right away. For the differences between the incommensurability thesis and the hierarchy thesis are differences that occur at the most basic level of understanding of the human good, and so any constructive debate between the two theses must first occur at this level. So, after first confronting a threshold challenge that any defender of hierarchy must confront, I will then develop the nature of the "for-the-sake-of" relationship that serves as the basic ligature of hierarchical ordering. This examination of the "for-the-sake-of" relationship will quickly lead us to the central question about the nature of the ultimate end, only after which we will be in a position to look at how hierarchy goes to work in some particular cases at different levels of moral decision-making.

While this response to George's invitation may not accomplish everything that George would require of the defender of hierarchy, I trust it will provide a first rough sketch of the form an adequate response to his invitation must take.

## A Threshold Challenge

In his recent book, *Natural Law and Practical Rationality*, a natural law defense which, like George's, reposes upon the incommensurability thesis, Mark Murphy reads both George and John Finnis as issuing the following threshold challenge to any defender of hierarchy. Any defender of hierarchy must show first either that the incommensurability thesis applied to the basic goods is false, or that incommensurability is consistent with hierarchy.[10]

So to take up the first part of the disjunction: is it the case that the defender of hierarchy must reject the incommensurability thesis as false? The answer, perhaps surprisingly, is no. The incommensurability thesis is, in fact, not false if by incommensurability we mean that intrinsically valuable goods, at least, cannot be reduced to a single genus. This is one of the points pressed by Aristotle against Plato's Form of the Good in the sixth chapter of Book I of the *Nicomachean Ethics*. The Platonists themselves, Aristotle says, do not postulate a single form for classes of things in which prior and posterior are found, as is the case with numbers. While there are forms for individual numbers, there is no form of number itself, because the class of numbers is comprised of various natures ordered to each other and to a first. And so it is with the good. Goodness manifests itself across the categories: there are good substances, good qualities, good relations, and so on. And these various manifestations of good, as with numbers, enjoy an order of prior and posterior. That which has goodness in

---

10   Murphy, *Natural Law and Practical Rationality*, p. 192.

itself, substance, is prior to all those other goods that manifest their goodness only in relation to substance. From these observations Aristotle concludes that just as there can be no common form of number, so there can be no common form of good.[11]

Thus it is perfectly appropriate to speak of intrinsically valuable (as opposed to instrumental) human goods as incommensurable. For human goods are not commensurable in the sense that they are merely different manifestations of a single kind of good. In this respect, they have no shared *mensura*. Accordingly, the hierarchical understanding of good I am defending has no truck with a commensurability thesis, or with those quasi-mathematical, maximizing strategies of practical rationality that trade on such a thesis, and which natural law theorists like George are absolutely right to condemn.

So, if the incommensurability thesis is not to be rejected, then we must affirm the other side of the disjunction, namely, that incommensurability is compatible with a hierarchical understanding of the good. Both Russell Pannier and Mark Murphy have noted that this compatibility has been implicitly recognized by theorists such as George. As Murphy puts it, there is a *tu quoque* rebuff to George's objection to hierarchy, for George himself holds "that each person is under a practical requirement to form a life plan that includes a subjective prioritization of the basic goods in his or her life."[12] But if the basic goods are such that they are amenable to subjective prioritization, then in principle, at least, there is nothing inconsistent in thinking that the basic goods can enjoy objective prioritization. "And if George asks," Murphy writes, "what particular requirements on choice are generated by the goods' naturally forming a hierarchy, the defender of that view can respond that it is the requirements on choice that would be generated by the goods' forming a structurally identical hierarchy through the agent's commitment."[13]

---

11  *EN* I.6 1096a17–23. Cf. *In I Ethicorum*, lectio 6, nn. 79–80. On this point I have learned from Kevin L. Flannery, S.J., *Acts Amid Precepts* (Washington D.C.: The Catholic University of America Press, 2001), Chapter 4. It is interesting to relate Aristotle's argument to Aquinas's analysis of the goodness of the human act. The species, or substance, of a human act, according to Aquinas, is a form/matter composite. This composite is considered formally in terms of the end (the object of the interior act of the will), but materially in terms of the object of the exterior act. The circumstances of the act accrue to the substance of the act as accidents of it. Thus in the human act there is an order of priority and posteriority, the substance of the act being prior. See *ST* I-II, q. 18, a. 6 and q. 7, a. 3.,

12  Murphy, *Natural Law and Practical Rationality*, p. 192. Here Murphy also references John Finnis, *Natural Law and Natural Rights*, pp. 100–105. See also Russell Pannier, "Finnis and the Commensurability of Goods," *The New Scholasticism* 61 (1987): 440–61, esp. 443. Unlike Pannier, and for the reasons already given, I do not think it accurate to refer to a hierarchical ordering of goods as a *commensuration* of those goods, except perhaps in a very loose sense.

13  Ibid.

But what reasons are there for thinking that intrinsically valuable human goods actually do form a natural hierarchy? I would like to address that question now, as the next stage in showing how hierarchy works in providing real direction for choice.

### The "For-The-Sake-Of" Relation

Earlier I referred to Aquinas's description of the human good as a *duplex ordo*, a twofold order of goods both to one another and to the absolutely ultimate end. As Aquinas also says in this *lectio* of his Commentary, the order of goods to one another is made possible by their order to the absolutely ultimate end.[14] So in setting up the scaffolding of an objective hierarchy of goods, the existence and nature of an absolutely ultimate end must be established, as well as the ligatures that bind other less-than-ultimate ends both to it and to each other. Following both Aristotle's and Aquinas's procedure, I want to consider the ligatures first, the basic means-end structures that characterize the hierarchy of our objectives.

Permit me, first, some rather rudimentary distinctions that are nonetheless absolutely necessary for the argument to follow. Say that I have volunteered to play in a charity golf tournament. The actions that I take in preparation for my play – practicing for the tournament, driving to the site, the play itself – are all ends that I pursue for the sake of my overall end of benefiting some needy children. The benefit of the children serves as the final end, the term, of my action, while the ends subordinate to it serve as means to this final end. We already see that "means" and "ends" are relative terms. What makes the benefit of the children the final end of this train of action is that I would desire this end even if nothing else ever followed from it: such as public recognition of my action. All the other ends, however, at least within this train of activity, would not be pursued unless they were somehow productive of the end of helping the children. I might play golf for other reasons on other days, but I would not tune up to play in a charity tournament unless I was convinced that my participation would truly help the charity. Thus of any end we can ask whether we would pursue that end even if nothing resulted from it but the attainment of the end in question. Would I floss my teeth if that activity had no effect on dental hygiene? For most of us, I hope, the answer is no, and so we identify flossing teeth as a merely instrumental activity. Would we want to play golf apart from any usefulness it may serve? Of course we would. Playing golf is intrinsically valuable, a final end.[15] This example helps clarify that certain ends can be both instrumentally and intrinsically valuable, depending on the context in which they are pursued.

---

14  *In I Ethicorum*, lectio 1, no. 1.
15  Henry S. Richardson has a nice discussion of the way Aristotle uses counterfactuals in distinguishing final ends from instrumental ends, as well as from final ends that are also instrumental ends. See his *Practical Reasoning About Final Ends* (Cambridge University Press, 1997), pp. 53–57.

The "for-the-sake-of" relationships that hold between goods exhibit what Richard Kraut has called asymmetrical causal relations.[16] In Aristotle's well-known example, bridle-making is for the sake of riding, meaning that bridle-making helps bring riding into being and thus that riding is more desirable than bridle-making – hence the asymmetry in the relation. Moreover, because bridle-making is for the sake of riding, riding provides the standard or norm against which bridle-making is regulated. Bridle-making takes the form it does because the art of riding, the craft to which it is subordinated, takes the form it does. This is the meaning behind Aristotle's use in this context of the word *architektonikê*, "master-craft." The Greek term connotes a craft that is superior, of course, but superior insofar as it is an *archê*, a ruler, over the others. Politics, Aristotle's *politikê technê*, is the master-craft of master-crafts because it dictates to all other sciences and crafts both what is to be done in these crafts and how they are to be employed for the end of politics: the common good.

We are beginning to see how hierarchy provides direction for choice, insofar as the good for the sake of which another good is pursued regulates the pursuit of the subordinate good. A clarification on this point. A higher good regulates a lower good in more than one way. Commenting on the passage from Aristotle just mentioned, Aquinas claims that politics regulates practical activities both as to *whether* they should be pursued and *how* they should be pursued. But politics regulates speculative activities only as to whether they should be pursued, either at all or by a particular person. Politics does not dictate how a speculative science should be pursued – how in geometry, for example, conclusions should be drawn from premises. For this depends on the very nature of the subject matter of geometry.[17] So in the order of practice, at least, what Aquinas has to say about the relationship between politics and other activities seems to hold generally: lower goods are for the sake of higher goods, which in turn dictate whether and how the lower goods are to be pursued.

It is a good question whether the asymmetry in the for-the-sake-of relationship must always run in the same direction. Can x be for the sake of y, which in turn is for the sake of x? The goods of family life, in any Thomistic view, are ordered for the sake of practicing philosophy. But as a working philosopher, do I not also pursue philosophy for the sake of the goods of family life? This example quickly clarifies the point that goods are not ordered for the sake of each other in the same respect, thus ensuring that there is no true circularity in for-the-sake-of relationships. For while it is true that the goods of family life are ordered to philosophical wisdom, it is not true that philosophical wisdom is ordered, as a subordinate good, to the goods of family life. Philosophy understood *as employment* may be so ordered, but this is just to change the respect in

16   Richard Kraut, *Aristotle on the Human Good* (Princeton University Press, 1989), Chapter 4.
17   *In I Ethicorum*, lectio 1, no. 27.

which we consider philosophy. Employment understood as a mere means is always subordinated to the goods of family life, which in turn are always subordinated to the philosophical pursuit of truth.

For Aquinas, all intrinsically valuable goods exist in *per se*, that is necessary, relationships of the prior and posterior. Prudence is a superior virtue to fortitude, according to Aquinas, principally because it perfects that power of the soul concerned with the overall good of the agent. The hierarchy among these virtues is a *necessary* feature of the human good, such that a conception of fortitude not put in the service of and regulated by prudence would not be the genuine article at all. In the film *The Perfect Storm* the members of a fishing crew lose their lives pursuing a catch straight into the teeth of the storm of the century. True, they are down-on-their-luck fishermen, desperately in need of a good catch. But clearly it was not worth risking their lives to catch even more fish than they had already caught. The daring quality they exhibit in battling the storm is in some sense impressive, the film's marketing company may describe it as "courageous," but in the absence of prudence we can't admit that it's anything other than recklessness.[18]

We may conclude from this that the very character of intrinsically valuable goods depends upon how they are subordinated to and regulated by goods superior in the hierarchy. This is why to speak of "basic goods" – even in their instantiations – as discrete, incommensurable items (George employs the unfortunate metaphor of 'quanta'[19]) is not to speak of real goods at all, but only of generic, ghostly entities incapable of directing choice. Once again, it is a feature of intrinsically valuable goods (at least, of all but one of them) that they are instrumental to higher goods, and that the whether and how of their pursuit are guided by these higher goods. We simply don't fully understand the good of "life," for example, until we understand that in certain circumstances it must be sacrificed, subordinated to, the familial or political common good.

Of course, George and others attempt to get around this difficulty by invoking the notion of "integral human fulfillment," an appeal to an ultimate end that brings some definition to the basic goods and provides the ultimate direction for, and justification of, human choice. Hence it is opportune at this juncture of the argument to consider the role of the ultimate end in serving as the *principium* of the hierarchy of goods.

Before that, however, a brief digest of points made so far.

---

18   This kind of argument is developed in Alasdair MacIntyre's defense of a teleological, as opposed to a functionalist, account of virtue in his "*SÇphrosun*': How a Virtue Can Become Socially Disruptive," in *Midwest Studies in Philosophy* XIII (1988): pp. 1–11.

19   George, *In Defense of the Natural Law*, p. 96. See also Russell Hittinger, "After MacIntyre: Natural Law Theory, Virtue Ethics, and Eudaimonia," *International Philosophical Quarterly* (December 1989): pp. 449–61.

First, the Thomistic understanding of hierarchy affirms that *intrinsically valuable human goods are heterogeneous in character*. These goods are thus not commensurable, such that the many goods we perceive are *merely* instantiations of, or instrumentally useful for, the absolutely ultimate end, the one and only intrinsically valuable human good and the single measure of goodness. This kind of commensuration has been roundly repudiated by contemporary writers and rightly so.

Second, *the incommensurability or heterogeneity of the human good, its resistance to any form of commensuration, does not preclude its being ordered according to priority and posteriority*. All of being is ordered to substance, an order which is manifest in the moral sphere in the way that the different substantial human goods are ordered to that which is the substance of the human good in the most perfect sense: the absolutely ultimate end.

Third, *within this hierarchical ordering of goods there are many different goods which are ultimate or final, though in a qualified sense*. But the fact that they are ultimate in any sense means that they are desirable for their own sake. We don't just desire them because they help us achieve the absolutely ultimate end (though they do that, too); we don't wholly reduce them to instrumental goods simply because they have an instrumental aspect to them.

### The Hierarchy of Happinesses

It is a commonplace of much contemporary Aristotelian scholarship and even some Thomistic that the for-the-sake-of relationship that I have been arguing is essential to an understanding of the human good cannot be applied to the ultimate end itself. In his book on *Aquinas*, for example, John Finnis speaks of *beatitudo* as a basic good. "But this turns out to be," he writes, "not so much an item to be added to the list of basic human goods, as rather a kind of synthesis of them: [namely] satisfaction of all intelligent desires and participation in all the basic human goods…and thus a fulfillment which is complete and integral."[20] Elsewhere Finnis describes imperfect beatitude, at least, as "the good of complete reasonableness in one's willing of human goods."[21]

Roughly, then, we might summarize this view of the ultimate end as the activity of pursuing the basic goods in as unified a manner as possible, according to the hierarchy we have constructed for ourselves, without in any way disrespecting the intrinsic value of any of the goods by manipulating it as a mere means. To act in this way is to act both from reason and from virtue – and, apparently, "for the sake of" the ultimate end of imperfect happiness.

---

20   John Finnis, *Aquinas: Moral, Political and Legal Theory* (Oxford University Press, 1998), pp. 85–86.

21   Ibid., p. 108.

But it is important not to confuse the "for-the-sake-of" relationship with this inclusive relationship described by Finnis. By an inclusive relationship I mean a formal relationship of part to whole, as when we say putting is a part of golf, or the pursuit of play is a part of imperfect happiness. To say that putting is "for the sake of" golf makes hash out of the phrase "for the sake of," if all that is meant is that putting is a constituent part of golf. True enough, putting is a part of golf if we are considering the constituent items and activities that go to make up a game of golf, like driving, chipping and cursing. This kind of consideration is formal in character. But within this formal consideration putting is in no meaningful sense "for the sake of" golf; for putting in this sense *simply is* golf. So, the only meaningful use of the phrase "for the sake of" is when the phrase is meant to say that one thing helps bring some other thing extrinsic to it into being and is regulated by it. Therefore, my two-putt on 17 is good insofar as it serves as the end of my desire to play golf on a Saturday morning; "putting" in this sense is the goal of an entire train of instrumental activities "for the sake of" landing me on the golf course. My two-putt on 17 is also good in an instrumental sense, insofar as it brings about, is "for the sake of," my continued play on 18 and my over-arching goal of finishing my round in the lowest possible number of strokes. "Putting" has an instrumental relationship to the good of "golf," if by "golf" we mean the completion of my round, not the game formally considered.[22]

My point here is not to deny that it's meaningful to say, "Happiness for me is my family, my friends, my work, my recreational activities, my devotion to God, etc." We speak in this way all the time. My point, rather, is that this way of speaking does not refer to the primary sense of happiness, the sense which *establishes* the *per se* order of multiple goods according to prior and posterior – and this sense, of course, is founded upon God. Without this sense of happiness, no other sense of happiness (including the reference to a set of constituents thereof), and more importantly, no direction for choice, is possible.

I have no intention of canvassing here Aquinas's arguments for the very existence of an ultimate end, for why the ultimate end must be one and not many, and the dialectical arguments he uses to manifest the nature of both imperfect and perfect happiness. Instead, I simply want to highlight some features of the arguments Aquinas develops in pursuing these questions.

First, when Aquinas argues in article 4, question 1 of the *Prima secundae* that there must be an ultimate end of human life, he stakes his claim on the fact that for human action even to get up and running, whether in the order of inten-

---

22  These remarks can also be taken as a partial rebuttal of J. L. Ackrill's inclusivist understanding of Aristotle's view of the good. See Ackrill's "Aristotle on *Eudaimonia*," reprinted in Amélie Rorty, ed., *Essays on Aristotle's Ethics* (Los Angeles, CA: University of California Press, 1980).

tion or of execution, there must be a *per se* order of ends culminating in an absolutely first, absolutely ultimate, end. And when in the next article Aquinas proves that the absolutely ultimate end must be single, he tells us that the hierarchy of "for-the-sake-of" relationships must culminate in a final end that is never for the sake of some other good, and thus serves to regulate every other good in the hierarchy which is, in some respect (though not in every respect) instrumental to it. In the *sed contra* of article 5 Aquinas glosses Matthew 6:24 ("No man can serve two masters") as a way of saying that no one can pursue two final ends *not ordered to one another*; that is, not situated within a network of "for-the-sake-of" relationships.

Apropos of this latter text Germain Grisez has argued that "[o]f course, in choosing, one seeks a good loved for itself. In this sense, one always acts for an ultimate end – that is, an end not pursued as a means to some ulterior end. But an ultimate end in this sense need not be the complete good of the human person, as Thomas assumed when he tried to prove that one's will cannot be directed simultaneously to two or more ultimate ends" [Grisez's citation is then to *ST* I-II, q. 1, a. 5].[23] But it is not the case that Aquinas didn't understand that there could be many final ends, each one imperfectly fulfilling of the human person. It is rather that he understood these less-than-absolutely final ends as existing in a *duplex ordo* to one another and to an absolutely ultimate end, in the absence of which no pursuit of any final end would ever occur. For what gets human action up and going is the pursuit of complete fulfillment of desire.

Human happiness is thus best defined as a unity in multiplicity, and this in more than one sense. As governed by the precepts of the natural law, our pursuit of happiness is always for something that is, in some sense, common. But as there are degrees of finality or perfection in goods in general, so there will be degrees of perfection in common good. There is only one common good that most perfectly satisfies the criteria of human happiness, and that is, strictly speaking, God himself. Accordingly, in the most perfect sense happiness is union with God in the next life; far less perfectly, it is contemplation of God in this life. But because we are not angels but embodied souls, this latter, mundane happiness must include the exercise of the moral and artistic virtues *as ordered to* the happiness of contemplation. This brings out the fact that a more perfect sense of happiness always subsumes that below it: all the happiness we seek in natural goods is taken up into and perfected in God,[24] while all the happiness we

---

23  Germain Grisez, *The Way of the Lord Jesus*, vol. I, *Christian Moral Principles* (Chicago: Franciscan Herald Press, 1983), pp. 809–10, quoted and discussed in Ashley, "What is the End of the Human Person? The Vision of God and Integral Human Fulfillment," pp. 68–69, especially.

24  It is interesting to note in this regard that for Aquinas even the moral virtues endure after this life, albeit in their formal, rather than material nature. See *ST* I-II, q. 67, a. 1. Something analogous holds with the intellectual virtues, including, I assume, the virtues of art (*ST* I-II, q. 67, a. 2).

seek in the practice of moral and artistic virtue is taken up into and perfected in the life of contemplation.

Observations such as these customarily elicit two objections. The first objection I shall call, borrowing a phrase from Russell Pannier, the "personal destinies" objection. Does this objective hierarchy of goods leave any place for personal predilection and native talent in determining one's happiness?

What the good obliges me to do is structure my commitments according to the hierarchical framework of goods, rules and virtues. However, the basic framework can be instantiated, can be *determined* by the judgment of prudence, in myriad ways. I may possess neither the desire, talent nor opportunity to be a statesman, but justice will still be a good that I am bound to pursue. I may have neither the talent nor opportunity to study philosophy in a rigorous way, but I can still make contemplative activity the highest and best good that I pursue, perhaps by reflection on works of art, or conversations with friends, or by prayer. This solution to the problem does not deny – indeed, it does everything to affirm – a hierarchy of offices and duties that is not the production of individual choice. The wider a common good a particular office or duty looks after, the more divine-like and honorable it is.[25] Yet again, this does not mean that the lives of those who occupy lower offices are diminished. They are perfect in their own order, and in their perfection make a necessary contribution to the common good of the whole.

But what then of the related, "domination" objection? If contemplation and religious observance are the best goods, why shouldn't I spend all my time with them? To answer this we need to recall that higher goods in a hierarchy do not undermine the intrinsic goodness of the goods subordinate to them. My obligation to honor my parents, for instance, binds me to the goods of family life in a way that is constitutive of my happiness. My other obligation to honor God in the practice of the virtue of religion is not a rival to this obligation, even while it remains the more important obligation. The natural law in no way requires that I pursue religious acts to the exclusion of all other obligations. The natural law only demands that the religious obligation is given foremost respect in the tailoring of the hierarchy to my individual circumstances. In fact, it would be contrary to the proper understanding of my religious obligation if I did not understand the way in which it depends upon my lower obligations. The honoring of parents and the enjoyment of the goods of family life not only have their own requirements, but the intellectual and moral education one receives in participating in these goods is required if the religious good is to be fully achieved.

### Particular Obligations

None of this discussion has yet identified any particular obligations. So in this final section I want to consider a bit more fully how the hierarchy I have

---

25   Cf. *In I Ethicorum*, lectio 2, no. 30.

been discussing issues in particular obligations, and in particular, I want to look at three obligations that arise at different levels of specificity in the order of practical reason.

Begin with the example of the golfer torn between his golf game and saving a drowning child. George's contention is that there is a moral rule that clearly says what one must do in such circumstances, and that rule is the Golden Rule. But what is the nature of this rule? What justifies it? George invokes it without explanation in the essay concerned with this golfing example. Finnis says more, at least about the rule itself: "The principle of love of neighbor-as-self," he argues, "and its specification in the Golden Rule, immediately capture one element in…integral directiveness: the basic goods are goods for any human being, and I must have a reason for preferring their instantiation in my own or my friends' existence." But why doesn't our golfer have a reason to prefer *his* life, and *his* golf, to that of his neighbor? The reason can only be explained in terms of hierarchy, and in the following way.

It is not at all contrary to my pursuit of a hierarchy of common goods to pursue some goods that are not in any immediate sense shared with the other members of my community. To go back again to the first *lectio* of the *Commentary on the Ethics*, Aquinas says that the whole which the polity or family constitutes has only a unity of order (as opposed to an absolute unity of composition, conjunction or continuity).[26] A family or polity is not a substance in the strictest sense, where every operation of a part is necessarily an operation of the whole. As a unity only of ordered parts, existing in "for-the-sake-of" relationships, one member of the order may have an operation that is not the operation of the whole, just as a soldier may have an activity (a furlough) that does not belong to the army as a whole. Nonetheless, the activities of the individual members of a unity of order are necessarily subordinated to the good of the whole. The soldier's furlough is ultimately for the sake of the army's victory over the enemy, insofar as the furlough refreshes the soldier for his duties. Indeed, the good of the whole demands that at times an individual seek a personal good both for his sake and for the sake of the whole. In the same way, our golfer's leisurely round is both for his sake and for the sake of his common pursuits with other members of his family and of his polity. But in those circumstances where a *necessary* feature of the common good is in jeopardy, as when a fellow citizen's life is in danger, a clear principle is invoked: the inferior, individual good must be abandoned for the sake of the higher, common good.

This golfing example deals with a moral principle at practical reason's highest level of generality, the principle that obliges us to love others as we love ourselves based upon the hierarchy of individual to common goods.[27] Let's look

---

26   Ibid., lectio 1, no. 5.

27   Key Thomistic texts concerning this principle are ST I-II q. 99, a. 1; q. 100, a. 3, ad 1, and a. 11.

now at another obligation, this one from practical reason's middle range. In the argument against polygamy that we find in the Supplement to the *Summa*, Aquinas sets down this principle: "Whatever renders an action improprotionate to the end which nature intends by a certain work, is said to be contrary to the natural law."[28] Aquinas then distinguishes that an action may be improportionate either to the principal or secondary end of an action. First, on account of something which wholly hinders the end, as a very great deficiency in eating hinders both the health of the body (the primary end of eating), and the ability to conduct our business (the secondary end of eating). Secondly, an act may be improportionate to either the primary or secondary end of an action by making its attainment difficult, or less satisfactory. I take this distinction to be a restatement of what we read at *Prima secundae* q. 99, article 1: our obligations under natural law bind us to whatever is absolutely necessary or expedient for the sake of the ends to which nature directs us. Any action out of line with this necessity or expediency is improportionate to the end, and therefore illicit. According to Aquinas, the principal end of marriage is procreation, and its secondary end is, in a word, the *bonum fides* shared between the spouses. Marriage also has a third, sacramental end, namely, the signification of the union between Christ and the Church.

Now when it comes to the question of polygamy, a plurality of wives in no way hinders or makes inexpedient the primary end of marriage. A man can just as well beget children from one wife or many. But it's a different story when it comes to the secondary end of marriage, the *bonum fides*. A plurality of wives, Aquinas says, while not wholly hindering the shared life of the spouses, hinders it greatly, as a man cannot easily satisfy the requests of several wives, and because the sharing of many in one office causes strife. And when it comes to the sacramental end of marriage, polygamy destroys the signification altogether. So, polygamy as a means for the sake of the primary end of marriage is not against the natural law, and clearly this conclusion arises out of the way in which the means of polygamy is a perfectly suitable instrument for the begetting of children. But polygamy is against the secondary principles of the natural law because it greatly hinders the secondary end of marriage. For these reasons Aquinas concludes that polygamy both is and is not contrary to the natural law.

Interestingly, however, the case of polygamy also helps us round out the argument by providing an example of where obligation arises out of the deliberations of prudence. In the succeeding article in this question of the Supplement, Aquinas goes on to discuss whether polygamy was ever lawful. Polygamy, he says, does not trespass against the first precepts of the natural law, because it does not hinder the primary end of marriage. But again, it does trespass against the secondary precepts, precepts that Aquinas says hold not always but in the majority of cases, because it greatly hinders the secondary end of

---

28 ST, Supplement, q. 65, a. 1.

marriage. Aquinas affirms that this secondary precept is framed by God and even written on the human heart, but that it was dispensed by God through an inward inspiration to the holy patriarchs at a time when it was expedient to dispense with the secondary precept. Why? Because the end of the primary precept, the begetting of children necessary for building up the kingdom of God, was, at that time, of over-riding necessity. So here we see how the decisions of prudence, in this case divine prudence, depend upon the discernment of hierarchy: the primary end of marriage regulating the pursuit of the secondary end of marriage in circumstances where the primary end is in jeopardy. The understanding, moreover, of the primary good's being in jeopardy depends in turn upon seeing how the primary end of marriage is for the sake of, and thus regulated by, religious observance.

## Conclusion

In this essay I have depended upon some central texts of Aquinas on obligation in order to show how the concept of a hierarchy of goods gives real direction to human choice. According to Aquinas, obligation arises first of all out of the recognition of an intrinsically valuable good to which we are naturally ordered, and secondly out of the recognition of means that either are necessary or expedient to the attainment of that good. Hence obligation depends upon recognition of hierarchy among goods.

Three features of this hierarchy have been particularly important for this discussion. First, that hierarchy fundamentally consists in asymmetrical causal relationships, in which a lower good is for the sake of a higher good in an efficient causal sense, but which also is regulated by that higher good in regard to the whether and how of its pursuit. Second, that this hierarchy of for-the-sake-of relationships culminates in an absolutely ultimate end that is not merely ultimate in an inclusivist sense, but which gives overriding direction to human choice by being the best good that we desire. Third, and perhaps most important for the debate with George, is the fact that in this hierarchy there is a wide range of ultimate ends that manifest intrinsic value while still being in certain respects for the sake of intrinsically more valuable ends, and most of all for the absolutely ultimate end. The instrumental aspect of these goods is an integral part of their nature as goods, even though it is not the only part of their nature. Still, when it comes to choices between these less-than-absolutely ultimate ends, between what George calls basic goods, the order brought into being by their instrumental relations is indeed what makes possible non-arbitrary direction for choice.